The slow traveller.

ernest.

Quarto

First published in 2023 by Leaping Hare Press,
an imprint of The Quarto Group.
One Triptych Place
London, SE1 9SH,
United Kingdom
T (0)20 7700 6700
www.quarto.com

Illustrations by Aidan Meighan

A catalogue record for this book is available from the British Library.

ISBN 978-0-7112-8232-2
Ebook ISBN 978-0-7112-8233-9

10 9 8 7 6 5 4 3 2 1

Design by Tina Hobson

Printed in China

FSC www.fsc.org MIX Paper | Supporting responsible forestry FSC® C016973

Jo Tinsley

The slow traveller.

An intentional path to mindful adventures

Leaping Hare Press

Contents

KROSSNESLAUG - 1954

Introduction

Rounding the corner of Norðurfjörður, a wide cove on Iceland's sparsely populated Westfjords, the thermal pool of Krossneslaug appeared as a jolt of turquoise water above a black boulder beach. Sinking into the steaming empty pool, I swam slowly to the far side and looked out over the North Atlantic. It was astonishing to think that there was nothing between here and Svalbard, a Norwegian archipelago in the Arctic Ocean, save 1,900km (1,200 miles) of slate-grey water. A gleaming iceberg with a single jagged peak, calved off the coast of Greenland, idled in the far distance.

As I floated in the 37°C (99°F) water, I reminisced over our past week road tripping around the Westfjords, Iceland's isolated northwestern peninsula where abrupt, flat-topped mountains tumble down to deep, narrow fjords. Would I have made it to this remote and remarkable pool – at the end of a 90km (56 mile) unpaved, potholed dead-end – had I not decided to savour Iceland over several separate trips, exploring one region at a time? Allowed space for spontaneous detours and the rich rewards of journeying to the end of no-through roads?

The Slow Traveller is the culmination of around twenty years of independent journeys and travel writing trips, during which I came to understand the rewards of exploring one place well, immersing myself in a landscape and culture and establishing a mindset that values curiosity, connection and authenticity. Over the course of this book, I will delve into this slow travel philosophy, exploring how we can travel more intentionally, from road trips and overlanding by train to journeys by water and on foot.

What is slow travel?

Slow travel is an invitation to explore the world at your own pace. It is unhurried and intuitive. It allows travel on terms that are meaningful both to you and to the people you meet along the way.

Although the name might suggest otherwise, slow travel isn't necessarily about speed or the length of your trip; it is more about deceleration and reframing travel as a journey. It is adding value to your trips, whatever their duration, by channelling your curiosity so you can form more lasting memories and enduring connections.

The Slow Traveller is an invitation to re-examine how we view travel. More important than what you pack, how long you travel for or your mode of transport, is establishing the right mindset. I would like this book to spark new perspectives, and new ways of seeing the world; to help shape a philosophy that allows us to journey lightly, gently and adventurously, while allowing space for curiosity and connection.

Embracing curiosity might mean exploring off-the-beaten-path destinations; creating playful rituals and routines to help you reconnect with a sense of wonder and enchantment in the world; or trusting your instincts to turn unexpected situations into memorable experiences. It could be venturing down a city's hidden backstreets such as Brighton's old Sussex twittens (p.126); or navigating an overlooked stretch of river by cross-country swimming (p.84); or trusting in an old network of narrow-gauge railways, through rough-hewn tunnels and steep ravines, along Spain's unspoilt northern coast (p.94).

Focusing on connection means taking time to scratch below the surface of a destination; to build a stronger attachment with, and understanding of, the places we are visiting. This might mean gathering over coffee in a local's front room; or sampling cheeses that have been slowly matured in nearby caves beside centuries-old cattle trails (p.50); or even creating your own personal, meaningful walking pilgrimage (p.68).

These are the sort of trips that allow you to truly get to know a place, its culture and its people; trips that prioritize human connection, opening you up to the kindness of strangers, to engage meaningfully with local communities.

Valuing connection might also mean reconnecting with ourselves: tuning in to our own deeper needs and coming back to what matters most. When applied back home, this shift in mindset can also help foster a renewed sense of belonging at home.

I think there's also a conversation to be had around honesty, both in how we view the world and how we portray it to others. To me, travelling authentically means to roam simply and intentionally; with no agenda other than to experience life in other parts of the world. Slow travel doesn't romanticize. It reveals how you can choose to view the world; to accept it as it is, rather than projecting an idealized version of it.

This can also include how you depict a destination to others, if you choose to document your trip.

I have often found that one of the simplest ways to travel authentically is to stay longer in a single destination. After all, slow travel is thoughtful travel; an opportunity to do less and see more, and to experience a deeper connection with each destination. Exploring one place well allows you to adjust your pace so you can absorb your surroundings and create opportunities for more meaningful encounters – something that is not only beneficial for us as travellers, but often for the people we meet and the places we visit, too.

Once slow travel becomes a mindset rather than a mode of travel, we realize that our journeys don't need big budgets, long trips or far-flung destinations to be genuinely transformative.

A post pandemic mindset shift

Slow travel isn't new, but it feels more appealing than ever; a tonic after several years of social distancing and restricted movement. As we emerge, slow travel is a way to take stock of what we have discovered during the big pause. It's also a less overwhelming re-entry into the world of travel, for those who might be still feeling cautious, and an intentional continuation of our less hurried pace.

After all, travel is more complicated nowadays; there is the uncertainty of cancelled flights, vaccination status and entry requirements. Maybe you have retained some caution about travelling on crowded flights or other modes of transport. Visiting a single destination, and exploring one place thoroughly, makes sense on many levels.

New travel trends are also emerging, informed by everything we learnt to value during the pandemic: a European renaissance of sleeper trains; more investment in cycling infrastructure; and a reinvention of pilgrimage trails, to name just a few. Many of us have also come to realize that adventurous travel can be had closer to home, for less money and less impact on the environment.

The importance of sustainable travel

The past few years have given us an even greater understanding of the impact our trips can have on the world. During the pandemic, we witnessed the environmental gains of vastly reduced air travel. More of us are looking for alternatives to cheap air travel, and are willing to invest the extra time, cost (and comfort) of travelling by rail, road or under our own steam.

When you consider that more than a quarter of worldwide greenhouse gases emissions come from transport, with air travel now the fastest-growing contributor to global warming, choosing alternative ways to travel is one of the single biggest steps you can take to cut your carbon footprint and reduce our impact on the environment. Slow travel goes hand in hand with this more sustainable, responsible approach to seeing the world.

Avoiding popular routes and choosing to explore at your own pace also helps counter overtourism, which can be harmful to local communities and to the environment, risking damage to historic sites and pricing local residents out of their own neighbourhoods.

Taking a slower, more considered approach is less disruptive to the communities we are spending time with; by travelling slowly, we are more likely to be genuine in our approach and consider our impact on the places and people we visit. In doing so, we shift from being simply a consumer to forging more of a two-way relationship with our destination. For travellers, this often means having more meaningful connections, but it also encourages us to spend our money locally, supporting businesses in remote regions and having a positive impact on the area we're visiting.

How I came to slow travel

My own journey in slow travel was very much homegrown. I feel like I have always been drawn to slower modes of transportation: to long-distance train or bus journeys and explorations on foot. My dad, whose own father was a railway signalman, instilled in me an enthusiasm for train travel and long-distance walking from a young age, which proved difficult to shift as I grew older.

As I embarked on a career in publishing, first as a walking route writer for *Countryfile Magazine* and later as a freelance travel writer and editor, I found myself seeking out slower, more intentional journeys. I also began to embrace the principles of slow journalism, understanding the value of honesty, integrity and down-to-earth storytelling.

In 2014, I founded *Ernest*, a slow travel journal made for those who value meandering journeys, fuelled by curiosity and guided by chance encounters. *Ernest* proved to be the ideal vehicle through which to dig even deeper into this idea, opening new opportunities to explore the world slowly. I am delighted to share just some of these slow adventures within the pages of this book.

Although my dad sadly passed away while I was writing this book, his memory lives on in my undiminished desire to explore the world under my own steam, and with care. It is now a passion I share with my toddler daughter, a champion footpath stomper and steam train enthusiast, with an enviable sense of curiosity and wonder in the world.

Forging slow pathways

The Slow Traveller examines numerous modes of transport that encourage us to travel more intentionally, with each chapter focusing on an element of the slow travel mindset as well as a mode of travelling, type of destination or experience.

The first chapter (p.22) explores road trips and van life, as a lens through which to examine the joys of intuitive travel. We discover how forging slow pathways, such as establishing a quest, driving to the end of the road and reading the landscape can help you to slip into a more instinctive mindset, letting your plans meander and your journey unfold day by day.

Slow travel gives us the opportunity to disconnect: from work, from our devices, from the news. But more often than not, what we are actually seeking is a different type of connection, and arguably one of the best ways to connect with a culture and its people is by sharing food. The second chapter (p.38) focuses on human connection and the simple joy of coming together to share a meal, uncovering customs that invite guests to gather around a host's table and partake of their home cooking.

Our third chapter (p.54) examines the slowest of journeys, the long-distance walking tour. We consider how the simplicity of putting one foot in front of the other gives us time to reflect and seek clarity; to reconnect with ourselves and find inner stillness, while also connecting deeply with the places we're travelling through. We also reflect on the historic practice of pilgrimage and discover a revival of pilgrim paths, which is giving way to a more personal reinterpretation.

If slow travel is all about taking pleasure in the journey, then travelling by water must be among the most satisfying ways to travel. The fourth chapter (p.76) discovers the unique perspective of roaming by water, exploring three different levels of immersion: sailing down sleepy backwaters; kayaking between islands; and cross-country swimming. We explore how the unhurried pace of a sailboat, kayak or canoe invites more mindful, intentional experiences, bestowing an opportunity to connect more deeply with the landscape, while getting rare glimpses into fragile areas of beauty.

The fifth chapter (p.92) is all about opening ourselves up to the unknown and embracing the idea of 'journey', coupled with the very special allure of long-distance rail travel. Travelling by train allows us to loosen our attachment to the idea of a perfect trip and to go with the flow. It also invites us to explore lesser-known back routes, flitting in and out of places and witnessing people's daily lives, even sampling delicious 'platform food' along the way – from *ekiben*, a special type of bento sold on platform kiosks across Japan, to delicious Indian street food passed through glassless train windows.

Our sixth chapter (p.108) explores the lost art of being alone: how intentional, freely chosen solitude can be a restorative and reflective experience, giving us space to be attentive both to our environment and to what is going on within ourselves. It also examines the enduring appeal of basic shelters where you can find this simple seclusion, from writer's cabins to alpine huts and Scottish bothies.

In stark contrast to these wild, mountainous landscapes, the seventh chapter (p.124) explores the thriving, frenetic energy of city travel, and how travelling slowly within urban environments can leave you feeling energized rather than burnt out. We investigate simple ways to immerse ourselves in the soul of a city, so we can notice the details and appreciate more.

In the conclusion (p.142), we discuss mindful adventures closer to home, exploring ways we can bring our travelling wisdom back home, to inspire us to live more mindfully and embrace the slow adventures on our doorsteps.

At the end of each chapter, illustrated guides explore practicalities and packing lists, from a foraging kit and lightweight luxuries worth the extra backpack weight, to tools to help you slow down in the city and what to pack for a cross-country swimming adventure. And at the end of the book (pp.152–156), you will find a slow travel reading list and trip planner: recommended reads and experiences that helped inform this book and may inspire your future journeys.

Closing thoughts from a slow traveller

Arguably, the aim of travel is to give us something we yearn for, but don't have enough of, in our everyday lives: more time, a chance to connect with ourselves and with others, an opportunity to pause. Slow travel brings us back to these simple intentions. It might take time to adjust to travelling at this gentler, more mindful pace, but the benefits can be transformative and long-lasting. Journeys made on these terms can leave an indelible mark on you; a warm afterglow that you bring back in your everyday life.

I sincerely hope that *The Slow Traveller* will inspire new perspectives and give you permission to explore the world at your own pace. Above all, I hope it allows an opportunity to reflect on what makes travel meaningful for you, so you can bring this to your future adventures, however and wherever you choose to roam.

Local traffic
only

On spontaneity & embracing the unexpected

Road Trips

When time feels so precious, spontaneity can become a neglected idea. And with the whole world seemingly documented – with all its must-sees and best bits ready to be ticked off – packing up a car or a van and heading off without a plan can seem, frankly, reckless.

But letting your plans meander and your journey unfold day by day can be the beginning of an unforgettable adventure. Our first chapter explores road trips and van life, delving into the possibilities that can open up when we trust our instincts and turn unexpected situations into memorable experiences.

Of course, spontaneity isn't always a choice. When you're travelling, even carefully laid plans can become unstuck; you take a wrong turn, miss a train connection or flight. You can never plan for the weather. At moments like these, it's easy to feel anxious, especially if you're used to planning every detail of your trip.

Reminding yourself to stay calm and to not despair at times like these takes practice. Over time, I have come to feel a weight lifting off my shoulders every time things don't quite go to plan. It's a strangely liberating feeling as you witness your expectations slipping away, with new possibilities unfurling before you like a newly laid track.

I wasn't always so relaxed. I remember a particularly alarming situation when a friend and I got lost on a sparsely inhabited Croatian island and missed our boat back. Overly confident that we knew the route to the jetty, we took one last swim while our fellow passengers packed up their things. Unfortunately, while everyone else was settling into their seats for the journey back, we missed the turning. We spent an hour staggering through prickly juniper shrubs as our shadows began to lengthen, a feeling of dread rising.

When we eventually found the dock, our boat was long gone. Only a private charter remained, the skipper untying her as we yelped and waved. Happily, the French-speaking crew ushered us aboard, and we embarked on what remains one of my most memorable journeys. As the crew passed around homemade moonshine, our fellow passengers

It's a strangely liberating feeling as you witness your expectations slipping away ...

(we couldn't share much conversation, but I assumed they were a group of salsa enthusiasts), drank, laughed and danced while a school of dolphins leapt around the boat.

Experiences like this taught me that chance encounters can often form the most lasting memories of a trip. Would I go back and change things, given the chance? Absolutely not.

Forging slow pathways

Allowing yourself to be spontaneous is easy when you're forced to act in an unexpected situation. But it comes far less naturally when you have the option to plan every step of your trip. Letting your plans unravel day by day means giving in to the fact that your hard-earned time off might not always go to plan; it involves abandoning the illusion of control; even accepting that some days might be downright boring.

When it comes to road trips, I have several tricks up my sleeve to help me slip into a more intuitive mindset. These slow travel practices and rituals – let's call them pathways – encourage me to let go of my perceived sense of control and to trust in the journey.

After all, slow travel is all about balance and pace. These pathways are strategies that allow you to slow down, which in turn allow more room for spontaneity. They are practices that help you create a balanced itinerary: they are a loose plan, allowing you space to pace yourself and make spontaneous decisions.

Of course, these pathways aren't finite. As you're reading, perhaps consider your own rituals, rules or mantras that could help you to shift your mindset and open yourself up to new ways of travelling.

Go to the end of the road

My first 'pathway' invites you to drive to the end of the road to see what you find there. I have stumbled upon so many unforgettable places this way, and it's an idea that was reaffirmed on a recent road trip to Iceland's Westfjords. Only 2 per cent of Icelanders live in this remote north-western peninsula, where sinuous roads run beside deep, narrow fjords.

The 232-km (144-mile) drive from the capital Reykjavík to Hólmavík is smooth, flat and achingly scenic. After that, the real adventure begins as pristine asphalt gives way to notoriously pot-holed, gravel tracks. When the roads aren't snaking over mountain passes, they skim the edge of the water.

Our plan was to seek out the region's thermal pools, stopping to swim in concrete pools at the end of lonely fjords and to clamber down to steaming natural rock pools cut into the cliffs, with the brisk Iceland Sea for our plunge pool. Along the way, we pulled over to watch splashing whale tails in the fjords; farm dogs befriended us and traipsed after us as we hiked up abrupt, flat-topped mountains.

Towards the end of our trip, we studied a map and debated how to spend our final two days. Should we close our loop at Hólmavík and

return to Reykjavik, or hang a left on the 643 road and follow it 90km (56 miles) to the very end, before driving all the way back? Upon a universal agreement, we chose the latter, and set out along a frankly terrifying road, dodging landslide debris on one side and a steep drop to the sea on the other.

But at the end lay the most memorable swim of our entire journey. Krossneslaug: a jolt of turquoise water on a black boulder beach, with nothing between the empty pool and Svalbard save about 1,900km (1,200 miles) of slate-grey sea. As we bathed in the 37°C (99°F) water, an iceberg, calved off the coast of Greenland, idled in the far distance.

Create a quest

Slow travel is all about adopting a mindset that focuses on curiosity and connection (something we focus on in more depth in our next chapter).

My second suggested pathway – to think of a quest – places curiosity and connection at its heart. You could see it as the antithesis of a bucket list, which might get in the way of more mindful intentions. Setting yourself a quest is more about coming up with your own unique theme, encouraging you to tread your own path rather than seek out popular tourist sites.

Travelling by car or campervan risks taking the most direct route to your destination. Setting a quest encourages us to take detours and savour the journey; and to be more open to our experiences and encounters along the way.

On the Westfjords trip, our 'quest' was to swim in the region's remote hot pools. On another trip, travelling by campervan along Scotland's west coast, I chose to avoid the more popular roads through the Highlands and to instead follow the little-known 'seafood trail' – a meandering off-the-beaten-track route cooked up by local

Slow travel is all about balance and pace.

producers, which connects crab shacks to oyster bars amid the jigsaw of islands and sea lochs that makes up the unsung Argyll coast.

Seeking out the region's finest local seafood took me from the clear waters of Loch Fyne all the way to the open sea. Along the way, I met schoolteachers who hand-dived for scallops in their spare time; beside a ruined castle, I tucked into scrambled eggs and *Bradan Rost* (kiln-roasted salmon invented by accident when someone left the kiln on too high); and I discovered yet another delicious dead end in the form of a wooden shack in Skipness, serving creel-caught langoustines with majestic views over the Isle of Arran.

Explore one place, well

Another slow travel mantra I observe when road tripping is to 'explore one place, well'. While I understand the appeal of epic overland routes such as Scotland's Route 500 or Iceland's Route 1 (the Ring Road), I often resist the temptation to cover too much distance in one go and instead focus on sections of these larger routes, stretching out my knowledge of a region bit by bit, like rolling out dough.

Exploring one place well is all about establishing your own pace. After all, slow travel is thoughtful travel; an opportunity to do less and see more, and to experience a deeper connection with a place. Exploring one place well allows you to adjust your pace so you can absorb your surroundings and have more meaningful encounters. This is not only beneficial for us as travellers but for the people we meet and the places we visit.

Avoiding popular routes and choosing to explore at your own pace also helps counter overtourism; it is less disruptive to the communities we are visiting. By travelling slowly, we are more likely to be genuine in our approach and consider our impact on the places and communities we visit. In doing so, we shift from being simply a consumer to forging more of a two-way relationship with the places we visit. For travellers, this often means having more meaningful connections, but it also encourages us to spend our money locally, supporting businesses in remote regions and having a positive impact on the area we're visiting.

Exploring one place well allows us to travel gently and adventurously. Gentle travel gives time to linger: to browse bookshops, to dawdle in a museum for a whole afternoon, to sit on a headland overlooking the sea, watching weather fronts pass by. It's a chance to take stock; to pay attention to what's around you and within you.

A quest places curiosity & connection at its heart.

Travelling adventurously means opening yourself up to uncertainty, risk and challenge. It requires you to be bold and decisive in your choices, to trust your capabilities, be steady in the face of challenges and uncertainty and to build inner resilience. Changing your pace in this way allows you to play all of this out on your travels, and then bring it back into your everyday life.

Giving yourself permission to not exhaust yourself by covering vast distances is also one way to offset travel fatigue – that feeling when you come back from a trip and immediately feel the need for a holiday. As slow travellers understand, 'there is always another trip'.

Don't set an end goal

When we focus on the destination, our journeys can often become something to be endured; a means to an end. However, when we choose not to set an end goal for our road trips, we free ourselves to be spontaneous, follow local recommendations and take detours at our leisure. We are more able to indulge our curiosity; we feel more free to follow signs on a whim or to visit somewhere simply because we like the placename. After all, you can't get lost when you don't have a destination in mind.

OPEN
UDIC

Taking detours to follow handwritten signs has seen me drive down a no-through road for miles to reach an honesty box 'farm shop' selling wild venison as homemade 'ready meals' from a wooden shed. On the same trip, I spent hours delighting in a 'pay what you think it's worth' antique shop (someone's garage filled with vintage crockery and ephemera).

Not setting an end goal for your road trips also frees us up when things don't quite go to plan. When the key to our hired campervan snapped in the lock on Scotland's remote Applecross Peninsula, we had no plans to shelve; we were free to pause our journey and await a replacement key. One of Scotland's most celebrated pubs, the Applecross Inn, was a mile's walk away, and so we treated ourselves to two nights in a proper bed and took long, leisurely baths with views over to Skye and the Isle of Raasay. Looking back, these were some of our most special days on the trip.

The flipside of being destination-free is accepting that not every day will be action-packed and filled with surprises. The truth is, some days might be downright boring. You might also doubt yourself and imagine all the other things you could be doing with your time. But hang tight and remind yourself that those spontaneous moments that stay with you long after you return cannot be rushed or staged.

If you ever find yourself at a total loss, ask yourself: 'If it were entirely up to me, how would I spend my day?' Rather than focusing on what others have done before you, or what you might miss out on, check in with what you need most at that time. Perhaps it's a 'day off' from travelling, so you can sit in your van (or in a lochside cafe) and read a book while the rain hammers down outside. Often the most indulgent days are surprisingly low-key.

Create your own rituals

My fifth pathway centres around creating road trip rituals. Whether it's tuning in to local radio

www.fieldcrestholidays.co.uk

stations, always bringing a special blanket or pillow or listening to audiobooks set in the location you're visiting; over countless road trips you can adopt your own rituals. These familiar routines can ground us as we move through unfamiliar terrain.

One of my most established traditions is to pull in somewhere achingly scenic to have coffee and breakfast each morning. And only then will I plan out the next leg of the journey. When travelling in a camper, the most appropriate places to park overnight may often be a layby or (with permission) a pub car park. Which is why my morning ritual involves getting up, throwing a jumper and boots over my pyjamas and setting straight off.

Only once I find somewhere scenic to pull up – a pot of coffee brewing and breakfast sizzling away in the background – will I unfold a map and plan out the next stage of my journey, tracing a route based on enticing contours or an intriguing stretch of coastline. As a meticulous planner in my everyday life, there is something giddy about allowing my journeys to unfold in this meandering way.

Road trip rituals like this can become an integral part of your journey, a comforting morning routine that gives a hint of structure and allows you space to be spontaneous with the rest of the day.

Read the landscape

There is a simple joy to travelling on empty roads through engaging scenery. With no turns to take, and no other vehicles in sight, you can allow your attention to drift as the scenery opens out in front of you, the line of the road drawing you ever onwards.

Being attentive to the environment you're passing through, and observing how a landscape morphs as you move through it, helps you to attune not only with nature but also with its rhythms, its seasons and elements. Sleeping in a van, or in a tent beside your car, you are never really 'indoors'. Over time, you let go of familiar routines, waking up when it gets light and hunkering down when the sun sets.

These tail ends of the day, when everyone else has gone home or moved on, present memorable moments, too: the delicious chill of early mornings waking up beside an empty beach, with all the time in the world to tread the strandline of seaweed and shells and see what else the morning tide has washed up; watching swirls of starlings at dusk; hearing the sound of nocturnal bird calls as you drift

Moments like these are invitations to connect with the wild.

off to sleep. I have stood entranced as a barn owl circled our field and I have awoken to the otherworldly calls of nesting lapwings. Moments like these are invitations to connect with the wild in a way you hadn't imagined.

Road trips also expose you to the elements. There is something strangely comforting about the sound of rain pummeling the roof of a campervan, or pulling up to a cliff edge to watch waves batter the coastline while you remain cosy inside your car. Paying attention to landscape, nature and the weather in all of these ways gives a chance to reflect on how these experiences make you feel, and what they bring up for you.

Our everyday lives follow certain structures – predictable patterns and routines that help us to feel secure – but that can also stifle our sense of spontaneity and adventure. Whether it's through establishing rituals or setting your own intentions or pathways, finding ways to travel more intuitively helps us to allow space to trust our instincts, relinquish control and give ourselves over to the unknown and the unpredictable.

Open yourself up to a degree of change, uncertainty and a measured amount of risk. I believe that finding opportunities to freewheel in this way is all a necessary and much-needed part of a balanced life. Road trips give us freedom.

When we loosen our attachment to plans and schedules, we also open ourselves to chance encounters. We become more likely to invite and accept the kindness of strangers, as our next chapter explores in more detail.

Road trip kit to help you slow down and connect with the landscape

Beach fire kit

A simple portable fire set gives you the freedom to cook on a remote beach or beside your vehicle in the most beautiful surroundings, while keeping the fire safely off the ground. Choose a robust style that folds flat for easy carrying, and you can use it for years to come.

Paper map

Make space for spontaneity and unhurried detours by investing in a paper map. There is just something so satisfying about unfolding a tactile map, then choosing the next leg of your route based on enticing contours or a particularly intriguing stretch of coastline.

Cast iron skillet

If you have the space (and it's not too heavy), why not bring along your favourite frying or griddle pan? Versatile, naturally non-stick and virtually indestructible, cast iron is the original campware; place it on the camping stove, over an open fire or even directly onto hot embers.

Camp coffee kit

Treat yourself to a fresh brew on the road. There is an astonishing array of quality gear available, from titanium (super lightweight) French presses and durable stainless-steel field kettles to collapsible coffee drippers.

Pocket handbooks

Choose a pocket handbook such as a seasonal almanac, birdwatching guide, or a natural navigation guide in place of a guidebook, to help you connect with the landscape wherever you are.

Rechargeable lantern

Sure, candles are romantic but a rugged, waterproof LED lantern, to charge as you drive via USB, is the one! Play cards when the dark draws in, light up your camp kitchen or hang from a tree for a cosy meal outdoors.

Basic cooking ingredients

Keep a stash of pocket-size herbs, spices and oils so you can buy fresh, local ingredients and prepare a meal at a moment's notice.

Journal

The daily ritual of noting down your thoughts on paper is a quintessential slow travel practice, which can help you adjust to the gentler pace of travel, declutter your mind and provide a treasured souvenir once you're home.

Wearable sleeping bag

Camping blankets – insulated, durable, machine washable – are a true van life staple. Choose a design that is adaptable, transforming into a pillow, sleeping bag and cosy robe for early mornings and evenings by the fire.

On human connection

The Simple Joy of Sharing Food

Slow travel gives us the opportunity to disconnect: from work, from our devices, from the news. But more often than not, what we are actually seeking is a different type of connection: with others, with ourselves, or perhaps with something greater than ourselves.

Arguably one of the best ways to connect with a culture and its people is by sharing food. Fortunately, all over the world there are customs that invite guests to gather around a host's table and partake of their home cooking. Gatherings like these afford us an opportunity to not only slow down and connect deeply with people, they also help us to gain an invaluable insight into other cultures. Because what is slow travel, if not a chance to listen, observe and be open to new perspectives?

Sharing a table

A popular custom in France, *table d'hote*, invites guests to gather around the 'host's table' to share in a home-cooked meal while getting to know one another. On a road trip to the Jura, a 360-km (225-mile) arc of sub-alpine hills stretching alongs the French–Swiss border, I stayed a night at La Ferme de Marie-Eugénie, on the western edge of the region. Owner Marie-Eugénie beamed as she greeted me, ushering me into the half-timbered barn where a vast wooden table was set for eight. 'It's all about *le table* [*d'hôte*],' she said. 'People of all ages and from all places gather to share a meal. It's different every time but it always works.'

Over dinner that evening, we settled around Marie-Eugénie's homely table with a young French couple and four Brits to share a delicious poulet de Bresse, a breed of chicken raised exclusively in the small town of Bresse in eastern France.

All over the world, you'll find customs in which friends, relatives and visitors gather to enjoy the warmth and company of others.

Just like French wine, its distinctive flavour comes down to the *terroir*, Marie-Eugénie's husband Dominique explained – a particular combination of soil, climate and ecology that's unique to the micro-region.

Later that evening, Dominique presented us with a cheese board bearing Comté, Morbier and Mont d'Or. The guests' shared passion pushed through any remaining reserve, each of us taking turns to boast about our region's finest dairy products, while Marie-Eugénie looked on contentedly from the kitchen.

There are traditions like this all over the world. I've particularly experienced this in northern regions where customs in which friends, relatives and visitors gather to enjoy the warmth and company of others can be a lifeline during long, dark winters.

In Greenland, *kaffemik*, which literally means to gather 'over coffee', is an open house invitation where people from the community drop by to celebrate births, a baby's first tooth or a boy's first caught fish over coffee and cake. Unlike the convivial atmosphere of a *table d'hote*, after some initial small talk, people often sit quietly together, content to be together in the here and now.

In Qaqortoq, South Greenland, Sophia sliced a bread-like cake filled with raisins and angelica, a common local herb, and laid it down on crisp white linen complete with her finest china. Seen from Sophia's rain-soaked garden, the town's colourful houses were like dioramas of Greenlandic life: cod drying on the porch; muskox skulls hanging over the front door; kayaks dripping under tarp.

As she poured rounds of milky coffee, Sophia talked of the culture shock felt by Greenlandic Inuits over the past decades as their traditions have been eroded. But she also spoke of how communities were becoming more confident and resilient, noting: 'We're a tiny population in a massive country but we're learning to come together and stand up for ourselves – and to feel proud.'

Partaking in similar customs over the years has shifted my perspectives in so many ways. During my time travelling around the North Atlantic's Faroe Islands, which sit between Iceland and the Shetland Islands, I shared conversations over food on topics that I might otherwise have skirted around or shut down completely, from faith and politics, to the tradition of whale hunting and 'harvesting' seabirds from the cliffs. Investing in these moments allowed me to understand something of the complexity of these cultural issues; something you can't get from a guidebook or a news story.

Shared experiences that benefit all

I also came to realize that it is not only travellers who are gaining from these shared experiences. This is something that really struck home when Faroese homesteaders Harriet and John invited me to their home for *heimablídni*, a local custom

meaning 'home hospitality' that gives visitors the chance to dine with locals in their homes.

'You don't get any more remote than this,' John said as he welcomed me into Hanusarstova, a traditional black-tarred farmhouse in Æðuvík (meaning 'Eider Cove') on the southern tip of the island Eysturoy. John told me that in winter, sea spray breaks over peoples' windows, despite houses being set 20m (650ft) back from the cliff edge.

'*Heimablídni* is all about inviting people into your home and giving them a meal but also sharing our stories, culture and traditions,' Harriet, a fifth-generation sheep farmer, told me as I sat down around their table. Wide curtain-less windows looked out over the ocean; their collie Lady pressed her nose against the back door.

Clearly in love with their home, they imparted its unusual backstory; how it was built using parts of an old church on Svínoy, a remote island in the far north, then moved to its present location by rowing boat. 'They dragged it up the cliffs,' John said, 'then reassembled it right here.'

A while later, we tucked into Faroese fish and chips – delicious fried herring caught by Harriet's dad, served with a curry-flavoured Béarnaise sauce, just the way her grandmother would make it.

'I grew up on a farm with my grandparents,' Harriet told us. 'It was my grandfather who taught me how to be at one with nature; how to sit on a rock for an hour and notice things. When I went to school, his dog would walk me to the bus stop and pick me up again. No one told him the schedule, he just seemed to know.

As we ate, it became clear that as well as taking joy in sharing their way of life, John and Harriet were invested in the concept of paying things forward. 'We want people to experience the simple, authentic life here on Faroe,' Harriet told me, 'to tell them a story about what village life is. But I've also always thought that if you welcome people into your home and show them genuine hospitality, it will make the world a better place.'

Opening ourselves up to chance encounters and the kindness of strangers in this way is at the heart of slow travel. It helps us to understand a culture: to meet its people and to drink, eat and laugh with them. Experiences like this might feel low-key, but these humble, human connections stay with us long after we've arrived back on home soil.

Slow Food

Meaningful encounters like this, which allow us to attune with what we value most in life, are also central to Slow Food, a grassroots and global organization that values traditional food preparation, delicious seasonal ingredients and considered choices. Slow Food is the origin of the entire 'slow' movement, which has since spilled into areas such as travel, fashion, cinema, cities, parenting and publishing.

Slow Food emerged in response to the opening of a McDonald's restaurant in Piazza di Spagna, Rome, in 1986. Shocked to hear about the arrival of the homogenous fast-food chain, founder Carlo Petrini joined thousands of protestors and handed out bowls of pasta to those gathered in the square. The protest was unsuccessful (in that the McDonald's opened as planned), but the event proved to be a catalyst for Petrini establishing a global movement, now active in over 150 countries around the world.

The Slow Food movement is remarkable in its breadth of reach, combining concerns about

It is not only travellers who are gaining from these shared experiences.

conserving the environment, tradition, industry and animal welfare with the importance of real cooking and the pleasure of eating.

The movement understands that food is part of our cultural identity, and that this heritage is worth preserving. It aims to enshrine the connection between the food we eat and the landscape it comes from. Slow Food means prioritizing what is local; rearing and growing with honesty and integrity, and always being mindful of the process. It also strives to protect regional traditions and to support Indigenous people in preserving their food traditions, seeing them as the custodians of irreplaceable knowledge passed down through generations.

For travellers, it is an invitation to eat locally and seasonally, to engage with growers and producers and to appreciate the connection between food and place. Not only does this support the local food culture and economy, it's a more enriching experience for the traveller. But how can we embrace these Slow Food values when we travel?

Seek out the distinctive

One approach is to bring the values you live by at home with you when you travel. If you eat organically, shop locally and support local businesses in your daily life, try to live by these principles while you're away. As tempting as it may be, booking an all-inclusive break might mean suspending some of the virtues you've taken such care to incorporate into your daily life.

One of the main focuses on the Slow Food movement is protecting regional and seasonal specialities. Seeking out these distinctive ingredients and ways of cooking will not only ground you in the distinctive landscape that produced them but could give you an invaluable insight into locals' lives and livelihoods, while supporting the industries keeping these traditions alive.

This might mean pulling up a stool at a *pintxos* bar in northern Spain (*'pintxo'* is the Basque variant of tapas) and watching the morning unfold over espresso and countless tiny local delicacies; placing an order for *boudin* (pronounced 'boo-dan') – rice, pork and spices in a smoked sausage casing – at a roadside stand in Louisiana; or sitting at an *okonomiyaki* counter

OIL MASSAGE

Human connections stay with us long after we have arrived back on home soil.

in Osaka, Japan, where chefs prepare a pan-fried dish of batter and cabbage topped with seafood, meat or kimchi on an in-built hot plate (*'okonomi'* literally means 'to one's liking').

Sometimes even villages or micro-regions will have their own specialities. In fact, in some places, local produce will be so celebrated that people may claim they can tell you exactly which valley it originated in by taste alone. This was certainly the case when I visited the Faroe Islands and spent a day with Gutti Winther, a charismatic chef with an infectious smile best known for TV series *Spískamarið* ('The Nordic Pantry'), in which he travels to all 18 Faroese islands, cooking local delicacies with residents while wearing a range of fetching wool jumpers.

Gutti had offered to take me on a mystery excursion into the world of Faroese slow food. As we drove north towards Eysturoy, he explained how each island has a distinct food culture: 'In the northern islands, the lamb tastes different. Farmers say they can tell which is their own sheep and where it's been grazing. Some even say they can tell if it's the right or left leg of the lamb.'

Few places have such a high dependency on the sea as the Faroe Islands. Ever since Norsemen settled the islands in the ninth and tenth centuries, people have sustained themselves on the raw materials of the North Atlantic. Little did I know I was about to be given a personal insight into the origin of some of these raw ingredients.

On Eysturoy, we pulled into a small harbour in Funningsfjørður and Gutti led me down a jetty, where I was warmly greeted by Steintór, captain of a small fishing boat, and hastily bundled on board. Berliner couple Francesco and Anja, who have bought a house nearby and regularly return to the archipelago to get stuck into Faroese life, were also along for the ride. Francesco, in his fluorescent oilskin salopettes pulled up over the world's thickest wool jumper, beamed at me as he rolled up his sleeves and rough-chopped fish heads for bait.

'Being out on the fjord feels like freedom,' Anja said, as we motored away from the jetty, explaining how she loved the endlessness of the ocean. 'Everything else seems to stop when you are out there.'

Waterfalls scored the hills opposite; we were all soon drenched in an icy drizzle. Being open to the elements, life in Faroe demands a boundless

respect for nature. 'People call this the land of maybe,' Gutti told me, explaining how one must understand the need for flexible timetables, and how it can be difficult to get people to commit. ' '"Kanska", they'll say: "Maybe".'

Steintór let the engine idle and worked with Francesco to pull up the day's catch. 'Today we are gathering one of Faroe's most highly prized catches: langoustines,' Gutti said, passing me one of the feisty crustaceans, as Francesco untangled the lines, methodically refilling the creels with bait and dropping them back into the water.

My face stinging from the rain, I took shelter in the wheelhouse where Steintór made me an instant coffee, tipping an inch of granules into a cup and filling it two-thirds with boiling water. At that moment, I had never tasted coffee so good. Hands wrapped around the steaming mug, I watched the activity at the back of the boat: Francesco in his soaked wool jumper, arms streaked with fish guts, laughing his heart out.

For me, experiences such as these epitomize what we are seeking through our slow, intentional travels. At the heart of the 'slow' movement is an understanding that genuine happiness often comes from simple things, such as opening ourselves up to the warmth of strangers or sharing food (or instant coffee) with newfound friends and hearing their stories. Prioritizing this vital human connection can not only fulfil our own deeper needs, it can also teach us so much about a culture and its people.

Connect with a landscape through food

Sampling local dishes and ingredients is a rewarding way to gain a deeper understanding of landscape, too; to join the dots between land and the livelihoods it supports. Because when we disconnect from the provenance of our food, we detach from our appreciation of place, too. Paying attention to how the distinctive geology, botany and even ocean currents affect the taste and character of our food encourages us to not only see new details in a landscape but to also appreciate how people have lived their lives going back generations.

Genuine happiness often comes from simple things ...

On a recent trip to northern Spain, I came to appreciate the limestone landscape on a much deeper level thanks to several insightful slow food experiences. A wild and astonishingly green region on Spain's northern coast, Asturias is a remarkable 'slow travel' destination. English is rarely spoken. People live off the land, mainly on smallholdings. Red-roofed homesteads and *hórreos* (granaries on stone pillars) dot the fields, swallows swoop into the eaves. Asturians have traditionally made a living through farming: rearing cattle, maturing cheese and fermenting cider.

To learn more about this astonishing landscape, I travelled to the heart of the Picos de Europa, a mountain range rising some 2,648m (over 1½ miles) above sea level, only 19km (12 miles) from the Atlantic coast. There I met up with local mountain guide, Nicolas (Nico) Barrena, beside Lago Ercina, which is one of three 40,000-year-old glacial pools in the peaks above the historic village of Covadonga, a place of pilgrimage.

As we picked up a path around the lake, a pair of glossy alpine choughs whistling

... dating back to Neolithic times, people would herd their cattle, sheep and goats from winter quarters in the valleys to the high mountain pastures.

overhead, Nico explained how the geology of the region is deeply intertwined with how people have lived here for hundreds of years. The Picos de Europa mountain range is composed almost entirely of oceanic limestone, uplifted high above sea level then eroded into vertical flutes, sinkholes and complex cave systems. It's these cave systems that are key to one of the region's most celebrated specialities.

Nico led me to a *majada* – an Asturian word meaning a cluster of stone shelters – and invited me into his family's hut, which sat in a maze of erupted limestone. 'The mountains make me feel at home,' he told me, as we warmed our hands on mugs of tea and listened to the rain pattering on the terracotta roof. 'Like that feeling you get when you return home after a long trip; safe, warm and connected.'

He unwrapped a parcel of cheese from his backpack and we sampled slices of Cabrales, a spicy blue made from unpasteurized milk that's been slowly matured in limestone caves on the Picos' sea-facing slopes. They make it in the valley, Nico told me, then place it in wooden moulds and carry it up the slopes to place in the caves to mature. Next we tried Gamonéu, a milder cheese made during the summer and smoked inside the huts. He pointed out the spaces between the eaves in his *majada* where the smoke would seep out.

The footpaths we were walking originated in these pastoral livelihoods. In a practice dating back to Neolithic times, people would herd their cattle, sheep and goats from winter quarters in the valleys to the high mountain pastures, a climb of some 1,000m (3,280ft).

After our pitstop, we followed one of these well-trodden routes, joining the *majada* to *invernales* (pastures) below. Asturias Mountain cattle lolloped beside the path, their bells tolling across the valley. I reflected on whether I would have paid these cattle, or the path I was walking, more than a passing thought had I not had this intimate experience to help me connect the dots between landscape, local lives and food.

Foraging and feasting for slow travellers, and new friends

Satchel or forager's bag

A simple, sturdy, cotton canvas shoulder or belt bag with plenty of pockets and a waterproof liner for berries, is a forager's best friend. Bring along a flask of hot water for brewing freshly picked leaves.

Cups for brewing foraged tea

Enamel mugs chip and may scald your fingers. Consider a Kuksa, a Sami design used in northern Scandinavia. Commonly carved from a single piece of birch, these robust cups give gentle warmth to cold hands as you sit with friends by the fire.

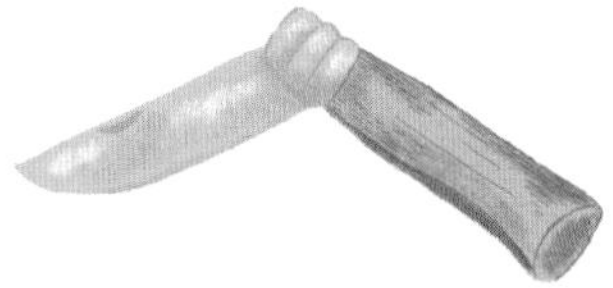

Pocket knife

The ideal entry-level foraging knife is compact, lightweight and durable, with a sharp blade that locks open, then folds safely away in a leather (or similar) pouch; perfect for prizing open cockles, pinching off leaves for tea or peeling campfire roasted chestnuts. Fungi knives have curved blades and a brush on the other end, for dusting your mushrooms.

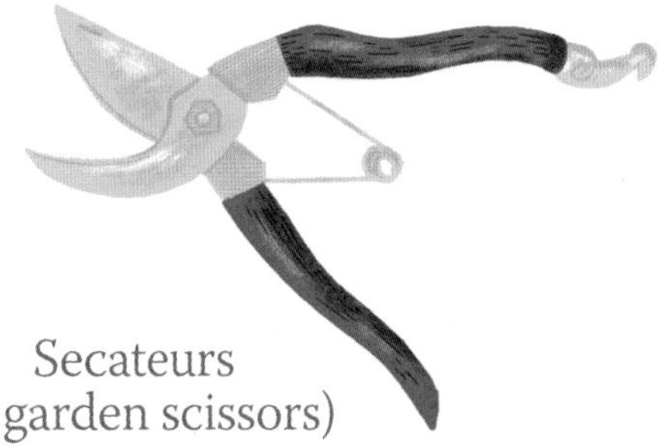

Secateurs (or garden scissors)

A pocket-knife alternative, these handy snippers will also help you harvest tougher edibles such as roots, branches of berries and medicinal barks.

Mesh produce bags

Gather soft edibles such as mushrooms and berries with these breathable, canvas or jute mesh bags. They keep food fresher for longer, and easily tuck into a backpack pocket.

Metal tins

A stackable set of metal tins is ideal for gathering. Alternatively, a lunchbox with separate compartments (like a Japanese bento) will do the trick.

Foraging ID book

While some forageable plants are hard to mistake with some prior knowledge, many have sinister lookalikes. Having a reliable edible plant ID book is vital; better still, team up with a local guide. Don't risk it if in doubt.

All-weather picnic rug

Keep dry and cosy while eating with new friends. Look for a rug with a water-resistant wax cotton base, which you can roll up and attach to your backpack.

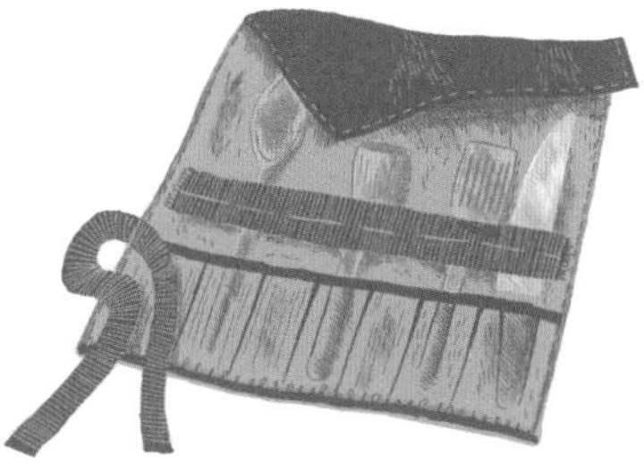

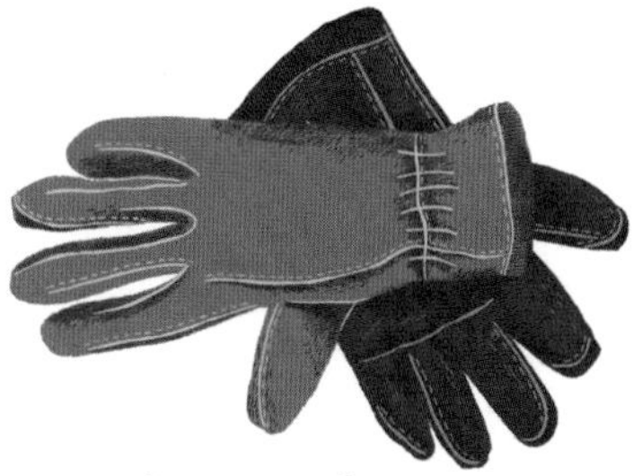

Utility roll

Often made of canvas or leather, with slim pockets, this keeps knives, cooking utensils and cutlery tidy and easy to find in your backpack. Hang it beside your camp kitchen for easy feast prep.

Gardening gloves

Don't let thorns or nettles keep you from your dinner! A pair of gardening gloves helps you ferret around in hedgerows and brambles.

On pilgrimage

The Beauty of Long-distance Walking Trails

While sharing meals and investing in the provenance of food helps us to connect with other people and to understand their culture, our next chapter explores a more personal sense of connection: how walking long-distance paths can afford us the space to connect with ourselves, bestowing a sense of freedom and clarity often lacking in our preoccupied lives.

We also delve into the historic practice of pilgrimage, and how a recent revival of pilgrim paths has paved the way for a more personal reinterpretation. We explore how setting an intention, discovering places that resonate and creating our own rituals along the way can bring a new level of meaning to our walks.

Putting one foot in front of the other

Walking is the most successful way of moving slowly through a landscape. The simplicity of putting one foot in front of the other gives us a sense of freedom like no other form of movement, allowing us space to connect – with ourselves, with people from all walks of life, and with the landscapes we're moving through.

After all, we predominantly live indoor lives, spending so much of our time sitting still. To move through a landscape, to cover distance under your own steam, is such a freeing thing to do. Slowing down in this way, forgoing the nine-to-five working day for a while, gradually loosens the pressure to be productive and allows your mind to drift.

It frees up space to finish a thought and clears room for new ideas. The benefits are particularly apparent on long-distance paths (or through-hikes),

The simplicity of putting one foot in front of the other gives us a sense of freedom like no other form of movement.

where you can be outside for weeks or months at a time. As your mind becomes absorbed by the basics – navigating, eating and sleeping; packing and repacking your bag – you gain a clarity not often found in our busy lives.

I find walking alone to be a particularly transformative experience. Walking with others can mean you are following someone else's pace, being jostled into conversation when you are in more of a contemplative mood or forced to stop on other peoples' schedules. Alone, you can not only set your own pace, you can also have moments with the landscape completely to yourself. And then there's the sense of accomplishment when you reach a summit or viewpoint and have the entire scene to yourself is something else.

Plus, you are never truly alone. Once a sense of stillness settles on your mind, you are free to open up a dialogue with yourself. You can give yourself the space you so desperately need, but don't often take: to daydream, to compose or to finish thoughts. For me, there's something about following a path that does this, the way it extends into the distance, leading my thoughts on.

Walking solo can clear your mind and pause the incessant chatter through which we judge ourselves and others; through the rhythmic pace, perhaps, but also through appreciating the permanence of nature. What are our everyday cares when we notice the longevity of ancient trees or enduring stone? Noticing these things encourages us to simply exist and to be, rather than to strive, or covet, or feel weighed down by our cares. We loosen our attachment to our culture of 'busyness'.

Finding your flow

Walking on your own allows you to find your own innate rhythm and pace, your natural cadence, which is much easier to achieve when you are not falling in with someone else's stride. You know when you have found your natural walking rhythm when you feel a lightness in your step and an easy propulsion forward. It's as if your feet find their balance without you even thinking about it. You also get a feeling of renewed energy, like you could carry on walking for days.

Whenever you reach this natural rhythm – whether it is through walking, cycling, swimming or running – something miraculous happens. As your body loosens, your mind quietens and almost floats in a way I can only compare to meditation. As your sense of time falls away, your thoughts begin to unspool. You might come up with solutions to problems, untangle a challenge that has been plaguing your mind or simply find new perspectives.

Perhaps there is something to learn here about finding your natural cadence in life. How often do we try to follow a pace that's dictated by someone else? Whether it's how quickly we meet a deadline, how vigorously we pursue a career, when or if we choose to start a family. Finding our own intuitive rhythm on a trail can teach us much about how we live our lives.

In her book, *Grounded*, outdoor therapist Ruth Allen explores the importance of movement in helping us to process emotions and find inner stillness. In a therapy setting, sitting still, she explains, can feel overwhelming, bringing up too much emotion to deal with. Walking in nature presents a less overwhelming way to find inner stillness and a much-need break from inner noise.

'Physical movement sparks our feelings and brings us into deeper contact with ourselves and with others,' she writes. 'Through movement, the jangly, stressed energy of the day can be discharged, and we can become quite mindful, letting thoughts come and go, with the only focus being the movements itself.'

As we walk, we can also pay attention to how our body feels; we can note not just how our muscles ache from the exertion of walking, but where we hold our tension, and how this loosens over days.

The physical feeling of walking also plays a part in helping us to shed the layers of identity that we wrap around ourselves. Because, after all, walking only asks for our bodies; for us to take one steady step in front of another. It does not ask for your relationships, your connections or your online persona; only you.

Time to reflect

The deprivation and simplification of a long-distance walk can also be liberating; you experience an unburdening. It's no wonder that at times of emotional upheaval – grief, separations and other big life changes – we instinctively turn to walking. The simplicity of putting one foot in front of the other, without the noise of the news or interactions with others, gives you time to reflect and to process. What does it matter if your phone remains buried at the bottom of a rucksack pocket for emergencies only, when you have your own path to walk?

Finding our own intuitive rhythm on a trail can teach us much about how we live our lives.

Walking can also prompt you to confront inner challenges you haven't previously had space to address. On a long-distance walk, you cannot escape yourself. There have been times while walking the South West Coast Path along Cornwall's coastline, when I have powered up (once, almost crawled up) steep sections of the path, playing out inner battles.

In my 20s and early 30s, I suffered from recurrent and debilitating panic attacks: moments of intense anxiety, dread and dissociation where I would feel an intense need to escape from wherever I was. Physical exertion, especially when on my own or in remote places, was one of many triggers.

Over two days of strenuous walking on the coast path, I confronted these demons with every steep incline, breathing through the intense sensations with each step. With nowhere to retreat to, I came to understand that there was no escaping. Wherever I was, the panic would remain; I would still be me, in this moment.

To move through the sensations was my only way forward. Hill walking became my trigger and my tonic; the sense of accomplishment when reaching each summit was transformative.

As a caveat, I am not advocating walking alone as a remedy for panic attacks; this was just one small step in my own long journey to overcoming anxiety. But walking can, in some circumstances, give you the space to work through tricky issues in your life, whether that be on your own or supported by the company of others.

Tuning in to the wonder of nature

Tackling a long-distance trail, especially if you are camping or staying in basic shelters, means being outside for weeks, if not months, at a time. You are more likely to experience a sense of wonder in nature. For a start, you get to see the tail ends of the day – the dawns and the dusks – which feel particularly remarkable when you're the only person there to witness these transient moments. You might experience enormous starry skies, watch brooding weather fronts move across an empty plain or ocean, or experience those precious end-of-the-season moments such as the feeling of winter sun on bare skin.

On long-distance walks, I have experienced many such moments of wonder – watching a meteor shower over the silhouette of sea stacks, walking through a valley peppered with glow worms and watching a thunderstorm roll in over the summit of a sacred volcano (before hastily making my way back down).

Walking solo also helps you to tune into the subtle sounds and sensations of nature. I particularly love sensing approaching rain. Firstly, there is a subtle temperature change, then the wind picks up and often changes direction. Bird calls fall silent. Then you hear the patter of raindrops on distant foliage, drawing closer until you hear them drumming the hedges right beside you; all of this, even before you feel a single drop.

Once, when walking in northern India, I tuned into the sounds of a predator passing close by. I was first alerted by a sambar deer barking a warning and stamping its hooves. Next, a troupe of monkeys let out rasping grunts from the canopy above, while 'chicken birds' let out high-pitched '*ka-tee-tar ... tee-tar*' calls from the undergrowth. I never saw the predator, but it was fascinating to hear the whole forest alerting us, and each other, to its presence.

Walking alone also allows you to notice the silences; and I say this in plural, because there are many different types of silence. There is the expectant silence of dawn, which you hear setting out early to make the most of the light – at times utterly still and noiseless, at other times interrupted by a cacophony of bird song. Then there is the cushiony, enveloping silence of fog; the air saturated as water condenses on the trees then drips onto the forest floor with an unpunctuated patter, as if the forest itself is raining. And the silence of a salt marsh – the creak of tilting sails and the crackle of cockles breathing through mud; a hundred tiny wingbeats as a swirl of waders rise over the marsh like smoke. You can tune into these and so many more quiet, still moments in nature when you are alone in a landscape.

Connecting with the landscape

Walking solo allows you to connect with the landscape in a deeper and more meaningful way. Without the distractions of others, you are free to observe the landscape slowly and constantly, as you move through it. This deepens your experience by making the landscapes familiar. Seeing a ridgeway or the shape of mountains through different lights and weathers

Walking only asks for our bodies; for us to take one steady step in front of another.

– sometimes vivid and pin sharp, other times obscured by mist and ethereal – lets you soak up the scene and relish it.

Walking long-distance paths might also present an opportunity to connect with your heritage. When my partner talks about walking the Camino de Santiago (the Way of St James) in northern Spain, he speaks of how he felt as if he was reconnecting with his Celtic heritage. Although not commonly thought of as part of the 'Celtic fringe,' northern Spain and Portugal were once populated by Celtic-speaking cultures and have a legacy of Celtic cultural traits; you can often spot Celtic symbology carved above doorways. I often wonder if my partner's instinctive connection with this 'Celtic landscape' was partly down to the geology, the limestone and slate, which is shared between some of the old Celtic regions.

When I walk sections of the Pennine Way (a national trail stretching for 430 km/268 miles across England's wild northern uplands), I feel something similar – it's almost like I am reconnecting with a displaced part of myself. This is the place where I grew up and where my ancestors have lived for generations, but it's also a place I never returned to, to live, in my adult life.

The limestone and Millstone Grit of these Pennine landscapes, together with the purple heather, bracken and peat, instil a feeling of safety and home. Wherever I encounter the same geology, I feel a similar sense of security. Walking, and connecting with landscapes in these ways, helps to foster an important sense of belonging in our otherwise displaced and disconnected lives.

Connecting with other people

When walking solo, it is important to carefully consider any risks, which will vary depending on the trail, the terrain and your own fitness and experience. Walking on established trails, whether alone or in company, is relatively safe; but you should consider perils such as getting lost, injuring yourself in a remote location, getting caught out by the weather or a natural event like an avalanche, or the rare chance of encountering dangerous animals or people.

Trust your instincts and know your limits. You can prepare by assessing your own fitness levels, your outdoor gear and your navigation and outdoor skills, then plan a route accordingly. You don't need to push yourself physically to reap the benefits of taking time for yourself in nature. Consider shorter distances, less remote locations or a popular route to build up your confidence. You might also choose to take a mountaineering or navigation course before setting out alone.

Once you've prepared and you are out on the trail, keep a phone charged and ready for emergencies, stick to designated paths and follow the rules of any national parks or conservation areas you are travelling through. And of course, always tell someone where you are going, the route you are taking and when you plan to reach your destination.

Plus, choosing to walk on your own doesn't have to mean forgoing the security and comfort of others entirely. In a small group you can walk at your own pace, gradually detaching from one another along a path, before regrouping at rest and lunch stops. For many, this companionable solitude presents an ideal balance that pairs the benefits of solo walking with the comfort of company.

If you prefer company every step of the way, there are plenty of benefits to walking in a group. And even if you set out walking alone, it's not uncommon for you to fall into a group somewhere along the way. On long-distance paths, if you walk at the same pace of someone else, you often find yourselves walking together for a time and then catching up each evening at the same rural campsites or hostel. You become incidental friends, joined by a shared experience.

You can often learn as much about yourself from interactions with these consequential strangers, as you do while walking alone. Often there's a certain intensity to these meetings and conversations. Walking side by side for a time allows conversation to flow freely, for you to meander from topic to topic and connect more deeply. There is more 'space' than in a face-to-face meeting, more pauses, more opportunity to listen or to allow your thoughts to wander.

Through these ambling conversations, we might hear more about peoples' reasons for walking, too. When my partner set out along the Camino de Santiago, he walked for a while with a fellow who felt disillusioned after a lifetime working on offshore oil rigs. Setting off from the far north of Scotland, the man had walked to England's south coast before picking up the Camino in France. After Spain, he planned to continue south and walk to Africa. He also met a woman who came to long-distance walking as a respite from caring for her husband. As she walked, he said he could see the tension held in her body dissipate, day by day.

Become a pilgrim

One mode of walking that brings people together from every walk of life and across cultures, geographies and ages, is pilgrimage. To be a pilgrim, in the traditional sense, is to undertake a journey (often on foot) towards a significant or sacred destination; to pay homage, atone for sins, give thanks or to bear witness to one's faith.

There are countless pilgrim paths across the world. Some of the most popular include: the Camino de Santiago, a network of ancient pilgrimage routes stretching across Europe and coming together at the tomb of St James in Santiago de Compostela in northwest Spain; the Kumano Kodo Trail in Japan, a network of pilgrim paths stretching across the mountainous Kii Peninsula, linking three sacred shrines and many other temples through bamboo forest, wide river valleys, mountain passes and terraced rice fields; and the California Missions Trail, which takes in 21 historic Spanish missions over 1,287km (800 miles) of path between San Francisco Bay and San Diego.

As with any other long-distance walk, you are likely to have the company of strangers along the way. Most pilgrim paths are also served by simple places to stay and eat. Walking Japan's Nakasendo

Walking side by side for a time allows conversation to flow freely, for you to meander from topic to topic and connect more deeply.

Trail between Kyoto and Edo (Tokyo), you can experience the warmth of traditional Japanese hospitality in *ryokan* guesthouses. Ascending the 5,500 steps to the summit of Sri Lanka's holy mountain, Adam's Peak, you can catch your breath at numerous tea houses, while Norway's 644-km (400-mile) St Olav's Way is served by medieval pilgrim farms such as Sygard Grytting, where the same family has been serving meat and fish from nearby forests, along with homemade bread and foraged berries, to hungry pilgrims for the past 700 years.

Walking ancient pilgrim routes connects us with those who have trodden these paths before us. But there is also an exciting revival of pilgrim paths taking place, where the intention feels far looser and open to reinterpretation.

Nowadays, pilgrimages aren't only undertaken for religious reasons. To turn a walk into a pilgrimage is more a matter of setting a personal intention or purpose, perhaps to dedicate your journey to growth, emotional process or to give thanks. As opposed to a purely devotional practice, it can also be an opportunity to reconnect with yourself, with others and with the landscapes you are moving through.

The British Pilgrimage Trust (BPT) is an important part of this reimagining, taking a non-religious approach to modern pilgrim paths. It is open and welcoming to all. The Trust states that: 'Pilgrimage is a pathway for practices that elevate the experience of moving through a landscape to one that is also an inner journey. The British Pilgrimage Trust believes that such a journey should be made on an individual's own terms, requiring no set beliefs. It is a pathway that should be open, accessible, and welcoming to all.

'Immersion in nature brings us closer to this primal part of ourselves. By paying particular attention to the land through which we travel, and the effect these places have on us, it is possible to cultivate a sense of belonging in, and return to, the natural world. In Britain we are losing our connection to this world at an alarming pace. We see pilgrimage as a practical

route into re-forming this connection. This opportunity for reconnection is open to all.'

Much of the BPT's work is about identifying places that might resonate with modern pilgrims, then piecing together the UK's many existing paths to create new walking routes that connect these places in a meaningful way, encouraging walkers to stop, contemplate and engage in their own unique, personal way. One of these new pilgrim paths, the 89-km (55-mile) Glastonbury Water Way, honours our connection with water – linking the ancient holy springs of Bath via rivers and streams to the mineral outflows at the foot of Glastonbury Tor, a place of pilgrimage for more than 10,000 years.

Creating your own pilgrimage

Pilgrimages aren't bound to established pilgrim paths, either. It's more about setting a destination and an intention and then finding meaning in the landscapes you're travelling through. Points of interest along the way should resonate with you and the purpose of your journey, but they don't have to be religious places like a shrine or cathedral; it could be an ancient tree, a hillfort or the source of a river. In fact, water is often a good place to start as they represent places where you can cleanse yourself and start anew, whether through immersion or other small and meaningful rituals.

A few years ago, Jack Smylie Wild, author of *Riverwise: Meditations on Afon Teifi*, took a pilgrimage to the source of the River Teifi in the Cambrian Hills in Wales, walking through Mynydd Bach, the bleak moorland where he lived for the first few years of his life. As he walked, he recalled his childhood and created rituals that held personal meaning for him.

In his book, Jack describes travelling through the landscape of his childhood, noticing, as he walks, the 'feral sheep; lichen-flecked walls; lakes – or llyns – like the crystal eyes of the hillsides; abandoned, graffitied bus stops; petrol stations fit only to refuel rusty Morris Minors and antique tractors ...' He reflects on his young parents, who moved to Mynydd Bach to join an eccentric community of 'misfits and unorthodox individuals,' and muses on the appeal of walking to river sources and their 'enigmatic beginnings.'

Arriving at a tiny waterfall close to the river's source, he places a piece of quartz taken from the mouth of the Teifi on a ledge. If the mouth of the Teifi, where he lives and works, stands for civilization, Jack ponders, 'then these hills around the source of the Teifi have come to represent for me those things that lie at the other end of the spectrum: freedom from thought, a rediscovery of enchantment, a wilderness of mind born of a wildness of place.'

Creating your own pilgrimage rituals, as Jack does, is a matter of discovering what holds meaning for you. It could be simple: walking in silence, sitting quietly in a woodland, making contact with ancient trees, swimming near the source of rivers or watching the sun rise or set on a hillfort or other high place.

A pilgrimage doesn't need to be long to feel significant, and it doesn't need to take place far away, either. Finding meaning in local walks can be an important part of settling into a new landscape. The cathedral city of Wells in Somerset has held a special place in my heart for many years. When I first moved to Bristol in my early 20s, it took me a while to find my tribe. And so every few weeks, I would take the bus to England's smallest city, where I would potter around the Saturday market, fill my rucksack pockets with local picnic fodder then ramble on various routes

out into the nearby Mendip Hills. It became my treasured time alone in nature.

Almost 20 years later, I find myself living a few miles from this place that had meant so much to a younger me. Only now with a toddler in tow, it's not like-minded friends I lack, but time to do the things I once loved. Recently, I met a friend at the bus station in Wells and we packed up our market lunches together and walked back to my new home. It was only a six-mile route along the East Mendip Way, but it felt remarkably meaningful to me: it was as if I was treading a path from one stage of my life to another.

However you choose to walk, whether on a long-distance path or on a short but meaningful pilgrimage, remember to set your own pace. After all, journeys on foot are not about how far you travel, but how deeply you connect with the landscape and with yourself along the way.

Finding meaning in local walks can be an important part of settling into a new landscape. To turn a walk into a pilgrimage is more a matter of setting a personal intention or purpose ...

Lightweight luxuries that are worth the extra weight!

Lightweight camping chair

Take a chair on a hike? Hear me out. On long-distance paths, a good rest can restore energy and increase stamina. At 0.5–1kg (1–2lb), a packable camping chair feels less like a luxury and more like an essential piece of kit.

Biodegradable soap

When hiking, it's important not to pollute water sources with regular soap. A tiny bottle of concentrated, multi-purpose, biodegradable soap can wash you, your clothes and your pots and pans.

Versatile neckwear

A favourite with long-distance walkers, a seamless neck warmer keeps your neck warm and safe from the sun's rays and can be worn as a headband, scrunchie, beanie, wristband or bandana.

Hiking socks

Spend wisely to keep your feet protected, warm and blister-free. Merino wool (or a wool blend) allows your feet to breathe, with anti-odour qualities for long wear.

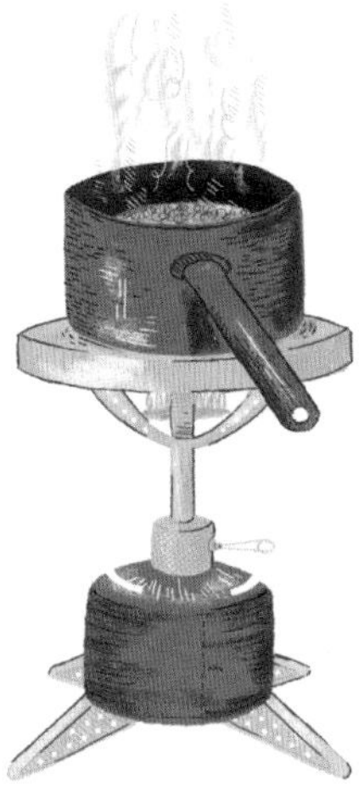

Down jacket

Warmer than fleece per ounce of jacket, lightweight and super packable, you will never regret bringing a down (or synthetic down) jacket with you on a trail; some designs can even pack down into a travel pillow!

One-pot stove system

These can boil a cup of water in less than a minute, operate in all weathers and cook up one-pot wonders on the trail. Their nesting design pack down, to be stowed neatly in your backpack.

Foot balm

A tiny pot of salve is worth its weight in gold for sore, tired feet. Use it as a friction balm to stop blisters or revive your toes by slathering them overnight.

Merino base layer

Fast-wicking, breathable and naturally-odour resistant, a lightweight merino wool baselayer, which keeps your temperature regulated, is essential. Opt for ethically sourced, non-mulesed wool.

Camp shoes

Kick off your hiking boots after a long stomp and slip into a lightweight pair of camp shoes (or tent slippers), with soft lining, quilted uppers and grippy soles; your feet will thank you.

Inflatable pillow

A good night's sleep is essential. The latest designs weigh a couple ounces and fit into your pocket when packed down. Choose a cosy down-filled topper for the ultimate lightweight comfort.

On getting there under your own steam

Journeys by Water

If slow travel is all about taking pleasure in the journey, then travelling by water must be among the most satisfying ways to travel. Roaming by water offers a unique perspective, affording you maximum exposure to nature while letting you see the shape of the landscape from a new and breathtaking point of view. In this chapter we explore travelling by water at three different levels of immersion: sailing down sleepy backwaters; kayaking between islands and canoeing down slow-moving rivers; and cross-country swimming. Each experience offers a unique perspective and insight into these enchanting environments.

The slowest of journeys

As a mode of travel, journeys by water are certainly among the 'slowest'. Travelling under sail, or by canoe or kayak, forces a certain slowness on you. It is an idle way of travelling, which allows you to adjust to the rhythms of the water and catch a rare glimpse into fragile areas of beauty: mercurial salt marsh, swirling kelp forests, tunnels of mangroves and rich intertidal zones where peculiar creatures – some spiny, some armoured, some leggy – take refuge. Water travel often takes you to places that are simply inaccessible on foot.

Of course, slow travel isn't necessarily about speed; it's more about deceleration. Lack of signal is a rare luxury. Being afloat offers a chance to unplug. In an age of acceleration and productivity, messing around on boats is a timely antithesis. It can become a balm for the over-worked and weary. What better way to slow down than to put yourself at the whim of the wind and tide?

There is also an appeal in the simplicity: cooking in a narrow galley kitchen while sailing; or packing everything you need for a three-day trip into the barrel of a canoe. These are all exercises in keeping things simple.

The unhurried pace of a sailboat makes it the ideal space for more mindful, intentional experiences: an opportunity to connect with the landscape, wildlife and communities. By travelling

What better way to slow down than to put yourself at the whim of the wind and tide?

at a slow pace, you can appreciate more; you are compelled to see one place, well. These immersive experiences are also great examples of a 'microadventure'; they might only take you away from home for 24 or 48 hours, but they leave you feeling utterly refreshed.

By slowing the pace of our travel, we reshape our relationship with place. It is an invitation to look more closely, to experience more deeply. Travel by boat leaves space for memorable, unexpected encounters with the wild: night swimming in phosphorescent waters, lying on the deck to watch a meteor shower or floating beside a sandy riverbank as sandmartins catch flies on the wing and nip in and out of their burrows.

Travelling under sail

Sailing on unhurried backwaters forces a certain slowness on you. With no engine, you are truly at the mercy of the wind and tide; you adjust to the rhythm of the river. You begin to take each day at nature's pace, waking early with the rising sun. Morning rituals revolve around cold water dips and brewing endless pots of coffee, listening for the morning sounds of nearby boats; hearing the creaking of cupboards, whistling of kettles and banging of heads.

Once you set sail, there is always something more to learn, and new skills to acquire. There are also countless quiet interludes – meandering conversations broken by long pauses, your progress measured by windmills counted and coffees brewed. As someone I met while sailing once told me: 'Once you untie your mooring lines, you pull the plug. You may be in the middle of nowhere, but you have arrived.'

In 2018, I journeyed through the Norfolk Broads in eastern England on a restored wherry (traditional cargo or passenger boat) named *White Moth*, exploring one of Britain's wildest stretches of wetland under sail. I spent four days sailing, eating and sleeping on board, travelling a distance that would have taken 16 minutes by car.

With no engine, we were truly at the mercy of the wind and tide. One time, we travelled so slowly, we were overtaken by a raft of ducklings. Another time, we stopped dead in the water. With nothing to do except wait for the wind to pick up, I simply studied the riverbank: I noticed a heron standing guard on a bone-white tree; warblers darted out of downy reed heads, catching flies over the still green water; I saw low-hanging branches dunking blackberries into the river, the surface tension forming little bowls around each one.

Sailing down gentle rivers like these encourages a slow mindset. Other than a few short bursts of energy to raise or lower the sail, once you set off, there isn't an awful lot to do. This leaves you space to notice things and tune into the boat's musical interludes – the metallic chink as wind fills a sail, the wing beats of geese overhead, the rustle of wind through reeds.

Evenings proved to be a low-key affair, unfolding by degrees in the warm and woody

WHERRY YACHT
WHITE MOTH
ROXHAM

Travel by boat leaves space for memorable, unexpected encounters with the wild ...

interior. After dropping the mud-weight (a type of anchor used in the Broads) and letting the boat gently rotate, we cooked up pots of Bolognese and drank tumblers of wine beside a five-octave yacht piano (a rare upright piano with foldable keyboard). After supper, there was little else to do but lie back on the deck and stare up at Norfolk's dark skies; point out satellites and squint at the glow coming from neighbouring portholes, imagining vignettes of life being played out inside.

While the unhurried pace of inland waters offers a chance to attune to nature's pace, the coast also affords ample opportunities for a slow adventure. A 'salt marsh sail' on skippered traditional boats on the Norfolk coast, for instance, lets you experience travelling with neither sail nor motor.

Boarding an engineless mussel flat – a flat-bottomed boat used to access shallow creeks to harvest mussels – you simply let the tide carry you deep into the otherworldly salt marsh, a wild and eerie landscape where salt and freshwater merges. Then when the tide pauses – hanging out to sea in perfect equilibrium – you can pause to swim in the creeks, forage for samphire and cockles and feel the mud oozing between your toes, before letting the outgoing tide pull you back into the harbour. Utter bliss.

Fuelled by curiosity

For an even more immersive experience, a canoe or kayak takes you where most boats can't go, letting you see the smaller details that would be blurred at higher speeds. You can explore fragile intertidal zones, reach isolated islands, enjoy close encounters with sea life and reimagine ancient landscapes. Being much closer to the water than in a sailboat, you also feel the tide and the current at much closer quarters. You're very much in nature; in its elements.

Over the years, I have experienced so many incredible moments while kayaking. In the pristine waters of the Isles of Scilly, I paddled over stone walls that ran down the beach and into the sea, giving captivating clues that these 140 granite peaks lying some 45 km (28 miles) off the Cornish coast once formed a single island. I have paddled through kelp forests, discovered ancient Scottish crannogs (fabricated refuges thought to date back to the Late Bronze Age to Early Iron Age), foraged for edible seaweeds and cooked cockles on a driftwood fire beside immense sea stacks.

One of my most memorable kayak adventures took place in the Discovery Islands in British Columbia, a jigsaw of islands between the western Canadian mainland and Vancouver Island. Over our three-day trip, we explored the fragile ecosystems of Surge Narrows and the Octopus Islands (so named because there are eight of them).

We paddled on flat, deep green water to explore bluff banks with stunted trees and lichen-coated rocks, while a bald eagle landed on a nearby shore pine, bending the flimsy branch.

Explore fragile intertidal zones, reach isolated islands, enjoy close encounters with sea life and reimagine ancient landscapes.

We disturbed a disgruntled seal, which slipped into the water, then popped up a metre away and snorted. And we found ourselves floating above thousands of papery moon jellies, which bobbed off the side of our kayaks and got stirred up by our paddle strokes. We detoured to a bizarre driftwood 'museum', a shack filled with decades of etched driftwood and cobbled-together sculptures – mementoes left by generations of passing boaters. In the evenings, we piled into a wood-fired sauna and leapt into phosphorescent waters, climbing out beaming with constellations on our thighs.

With the correct safety gear – and possibly a guide – there are plenty of adventures to be had with little or no experience. Personally, I favour meandering journeys, fuelled by curiosity rather than adrenaline. I have had my share of 'type II fun' over the years (an ordeal while you're doing it, fun in retrospect); nowadays, I seek more lingering and intentional adventures. And so when it comes to exploring by water, I tend to seek out creeks and backwaters, unhurried rivers and leisurely paddles in the still waters of a lake. It doesn't have to be daring to feel intrepid.

Messing about in boats

Slow adventures by kayak or canoe are also ideal for families. Picture misty mornings, wrapped in blankets, fuelling up on porridge and leftover marshmallows, then packing everything up into a Canadian canoe and setting off downriver; pioneers, every one of you. Later, you navigate shallow rapids and dodge low-hanging trees, with squeals of laughter as you run aground. There's nothing like moments of mild peril to bring a team together.

From *The Wind in the Willows* to Arthur Ransome's *Swallows and Amazons*, children's literature is filled with tales of adventures afloat. Understandably, too. Adventures by boat are a time for making lasting memories. Children love pottering around on boats, from mucking in to tie up ropes or help adults hoist the sail to learning to paddle, not to mention the simple joy of having their own berth or camp beside the water. Then there's the riverside wildlife to spot: herons! Kingfishers! Dragonflies! Otters!

Of course, this rosy picture might also include squabbles, splash battles, unexpected downpours and an inexhaustible chorus of 'are we nearly there yet?' When travelling slowly as a family, it's good to listen to your intuition and always be prepared to bail if things aren't quite going to plan. While pushing through some discomfort can build resilience, you also want this to be a memory that your children look back on fondly.

Over land & water

While navigating by boat offers a whole new perspective on river life, getting into the water and swimming allows you to completely

Cross-country swimming adventures vary ... You don't need to push your limits or find yourself in deep water.

immerse yourself in this watery world. 'Cross-country swimming' – a newly coined term meaning to combine swimming with hiking, cycling and even camping – allows you to negotiate both land and water.

An innovative range of cross-country swimming gear – such as 'swim–run' shoes, towfloats and a recently invented inflatable raft with a vast drybag into which you can pour your rucksack, towel, walking boots, picnic, a tent and camping stove (even a Brompton bike!) – along with a host of 'wild swimming' books and guides open up possibilities for intrepid missions on any scale. Armed with the right kit, you are ready for any terrain; to travel through forest, field and riverbed; taking everything you need with you to stay warm and well fed.

Creating your own expedition is achievable for any confident swimmer. In itself, this can feel adventurous; it doesn't need to be long distance or treacherous. After all, it's about delight, not endurance.

There is something infinitely intrepid about travelling across land and water in this meandering and instinctive way. To pioneer your own route, reach inaccessible places and build your own adventure. Simply set yourself a quest, whether that be to swim to a lake island and cook dinner there, to reach a secluded bay to warm your bones in the late afternoon sun or to swim and camp along the banks of an overlooked river. The possibilities are endless.

Cross-country swimming adventures vary vastly in terms of scale and ambition. You don't need to push your limits or find yourself in deep water. In fact, it is vital to stay safe and work within your own limits and capabilities. One of my most adventurous 'swims' was an incredible swim–float–scramble at Fidden Beach on the Isle of Mull, Scotland. We gradually made our way across three coves, swimming through turquoise water, scrambling over pink granite rocks and sculling over kelp forests; never out of our depth and always within wading distance of the shore.

It felt genuinely transgressive to walk through car parks and residential streets in our half-done up wetsuits and enter this secret world ...

A swim adventure might even be in an urban environment. Inspired by John Cheever's celebrated 1964 short story 'The Swimmer', in which a character called Neddy decides to swim home via all of his neighbours' pools, one regular London event invites participants on a relaxed half-marathon through London's finest parks, ponds and pools, with bacon butties and coffee laid on at the end.

You might even find watery adventures in unlikely places, as I discovered on a two-day swim down the River Mole in Surrey – a tributary of the Thames that rises in West Sussex before joining the Thames opposite Hampton Court Palace in Richmond. Our group of 22 wild swimmers met at a London train station and entered the river only a few hundred metres away.

On the first day, we swam, floated, waded and scrambled down over 7km (4½ miles) of the Mole, the depth of the water changing considerably over that distance. At times, we were swimming in deep, slow-moving bends of the river, absorbed in the rhythm of our strokes, and ducking below low-hanging branches. At other times, we would scramble over rocks or scull on our backs over fast-moving riffles (like baby rapids).

Parakeets, an invasive parrot species now common in London, screeched overhead, a blur of green. Pale blue damselfies flittered then settled on reeds. Swimming stealthily past a family of swans with eight cygnets was a thrilling moment.

What was remarkable was that the entire swim was within the M25, the motorway that encircles London. At times, we got so close that we could hear the hum of cars. And yet here we were, in this beautiful wilderness, which in its upper reaches boasts the greatest diversity of fish species of any river in England.

Although it was a local adventure, navigating a river like this felt like one of the most adventurous things I have ever done. It's even possible that we were the first people to ever swim along this specific stretch. It felt genuinely transgressive to walk through car parks and residential streets in our half-done up wetsuits and enter this secret world, then emerge many hours later – grinning, bedraggled and streaked with mud – into an eighteenth-century country estate for a cup of tea and some sideways glances. It was the furthest I have swum, and the most I think I have laughed.

How to pack for a cross-country swimming adventure

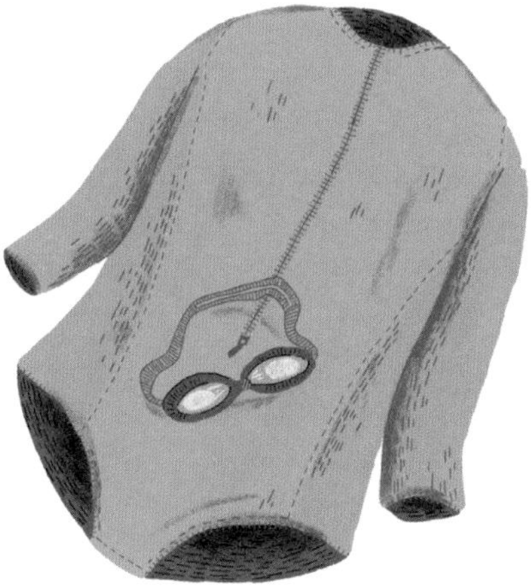

Thermal swimming costume and goggles

Depending on the water temperature, you might choose a full-body wetsuit or a long-sleeve swimsuit in a thermal fabric. A good alternative to neoprene (synthetic rubber derived from petroleum or limestone) is a natural rubber such as Yulex.

A towfloat

These inflatable drybags, which you tow behind as you swim, keep you visible and provide a reassuring floating device to rest on. And they keep small items, such as phone, keys and snacks, safe. But for longer adventures, the RuckRaft – an inflatable raft with a giant drybag into which you can pour everything on this page – is the ultimate cross-country swimming companion.

Swim shoes

If you'll mostly be in the water, a 'swim-run' shoe takes you seamlessly from water to the trail. For longer hikes, wear wetsuit booties in the water, then switch to hiking shoes on dry land.

Warm clothes

Merino base layers always work well, or a 'technical,' pub-ready shirt that is lightweight, breathable, fast-drying and uncreaseable – with lots of pockets.

Backpack

Some towfloats have comfy straps to transform into a rucksack. Or if you've opted for the RuckRaft, pack a roomy backpack to transfer your kit (and the deflated raft) inside when you begin your hike. Either way, pack maps, phones and precious items in separate drybags before stuffing into your pack.

Quick dry towel

A lightweight, highly absorbent and fast-drying towel is a must. There are some great linen and cotton alternatives to synthetic microfibres.

Suncream

Swimmers get hit by the sun's rays twice; once by the sky and again by rays bouncing off the water's surface. Keep your skin protected with a mineral-based sunscreen such as zinc.

Warm drink (and a snack)

After swimming in cold water, it is important to wrap up warmly straight away. Sipping a warm drink helps warm you gently from the inside, which is important because your body continues to lose heat up to 40 minutes after you leave the water (it's called 'after drop'). Sugar helps raise your body temperature too, which is why cake is essential.

Wool hat

An essential post-swim accessory. Wool is naturally breathable, so it regulates your temperature even in warm weather.

On embracing the journey

Epic Rail Journeys

There is a definite romance to long-distance train journeys, especially when there's a sleeper train involved. There's a sense of possibility and promise of adventure; that wondrous 'ta-da!' feeling of falling asleep in one place and waking up in another.

Unlike in a plane, you are not strapped in. You are free to wander, to stretch your legs, to sit down at an actual table in the restaurant car with metal cutlery and clinking glassware. You can sleep lying down, cocooned in your bunk with crisp sheets and a proper pillow.

More often than not, you also get a good night's sleep – lulled by the rhythmic side-to-side motion of the train, the derum-derum of steel wheels running over rail joints to create your own personal white-noise track.

When many of us are seeking slower, greener ways of seeing the world, opportunities to experience the many wonders of long-distance or nocturnal train travel are happily increasing. Once an endangered species, sleeper trains are experiencing an extraordinary renaissance, an increase in demand leading to more investment, with new services poised to connect 12 European cities by sleeper by 2024.

In an age of *flygskam* – a Swedish term capturing a sense of guilt associated with airline travel, literally 'flight shame' – more and more of us are looking for alternatives to cheap air travel, and are willing to invest the extra time, cost (and comfort) of an overnight train.

There is good reason to. Choosing alternatives to flying is one of the single biggest steps you can take to cut your carbon footprint and reduce your impact on the environment. After all, more than a quarter of worldwide greenhouse gas emissions come from transport, with air travel being the fastest-growing contributor to global warming. More shocking still, while many sectors of the travel industry are finding ways to reduce their emissions, aviation's have continued to grow rapidly. If left unchecked, a quarter of all emissions could result from flying by 2050. Aside from walking or cycling, rail travel is your next greenest option.

There's also been a zeitgeist shift away from always choosing the fastest and easiest route to your destination, with a renewed focus on the 'journey'. The antithesis of a round-the-world ticket or a whistle-stop city break, overlanding

Choosing alternatives to flying is one of the single biggest steps you can take to cut your carbon footprint and reduce your impact on the environment.

by train encourages us to let go of the focus on our destination and open ourselves up to new experiences and perspectives.

Be carried along for the ride

Rail travel encourages us to let go of expectations and embrace the unknown. Embarking on a train journey is a watershed moment: a point of letting go. It's an opportunity to loosen our attachment to the idea of a perfect trip; to be open to the present and to go with the flow.

After all, travel can be unsettling at times. Most of us seek simple, challenge-free trips. We want to arrive quickly, on time and with ease. Choosing to travel slowly, to not be 'the driver', brings with it a certain loss of control; an acceptance of missed connections, delays and cancellations. It can take a while to relax into it. Rail travel allows us to shake off this perceived sense of control in a safe and comfortable manner. Once we allow that shift of mindset and roll with it, we open ourselves up to new experiences and encounters.

It's a more flexible way to travel, too. Unlike air travel, you don't need to plan your trip too far in advance. You can buy flexible, hop-on, hop-off tickets such as an Interrail pass, which lets you explore 33 European countries by train. Or a JR Pass – one of the world's greatest transport bargains – which allows you to travel across Japan for 7, 14 or 21 days at a vastly discounted rate.

Travelling by rail also allows you to completely unwind. After all, someone else is doing the driving so you can simply sit back and let yourself be carried along for the ride. The rhythmic movement of the carriage, along with the slow unfolding of the scenery, allows your mind to drift. Watching a landscape spool before your eyes, it's hard not to feel present and in the moment.

It also gives you time to observe and reflect; to take stock. Some of my most productive time has been on train journeys, unplugged and offline, curled up by a window seat with a notebook and a pen.

Dipping into new places

There's a simple pleasure to flitting in and out of places, and witnessing people's daily lives, which you don't get with road or air travel, where you're either funnelled along motorways or dropped off at the other end, missing all the best bits.

This is something I learnt to appreciate when I spent five days hopping on and off the FEVE railway, a network of 1,000mm (39in) metre-gauge lines that carve an improbable route along Spain's unspoilt northern coast, stopping at over 100 stations along the way.

This unassuming little train, which runs from Bilbao (Basque Country) to Ferrol (Galicia), steadfastly resists the acceleration of modern life. Unperturbed by the *autovía* (freeways) that spring up around it, it hauls itself through rough-hewn tunnels, chugs up steep ravines and ducks beneath the legs of highway bridges, stopping at remote platforms in the middle of meadows and once elegant station buildings with cracked tile maps and a fading yellow paint.

GREAT WESTERN RAILWAY.
— NOTICE —
ALL PERSONS ARE WARNED NOT TO TRESPASS UPON THE RAILWAYS OR STATIONS OF THE COMPANY, AND NOTICE IS HEREBY GIVEN THAT PURSUANT TO THE PROVISIONS OF THE COMPANYS ACTS EVERY PERSON WHO TRESPASSES UPON ANY SUCH RAILWAY OR STATION IN SUCH MANNER AS TO EXPOSE HIMSELF TO DANGER OR RISK OF DANGER RENDERS HIMSELF LIABLE TO A PENALTY OF FORTY SHILLINGS AND IN DEFAULT OF PAYMENT TO ONE MONTHS IMPRISONMENT FOR EVERY SUCH OFFENCE.
BY ORDER.

25
naturaplan
Naturel. Juste. Bon.

Beautifully isolated and content with its own slow progress, the FEVE immerses the unhurried in an astonishingly green region of untamed mountains, hearty food and authentic people.

Departing from Santander, I shared a carriage with commuters, tapping away on their phones or snoozing against windows. But it didn't take long before the city fringes were replaced by low hills topped with white stone churches and willow beds that blurred beside a shallow river. As seats slowly emptied, and the stations began to get smaller, the train carried me on a wilder journey. Canoeists navigated rapids of the river below, and locals quaffed cider and chatted on the secluded platforms. My fellow passengers were no longer commuters, but villagers on their way to the butchers or to take their dog to the vet.

'On a city train, commuters will sit as far away as they can from other people,' Manolo, a former biologist and now hotelier, told me one day, while we waited for a delayed connection. 'On the FEVE, if there's one person in a carriage, you'll sit right next to them. It's a chance to meet other local people and to access the culture of nearby towns. It helps us realize we are not completely apart from the world.'

Explore the back routes

Another benefit of rail travel is being able to explore lesser-known back routes, both in the city and in the wildest of landscapes. Historically, railways were engineered to follow the contours of the land, meaning that tracks often followed natural features such as rivers and canyons. On routes like these, I can't help but be captivated by the tenacity of railway engineering, the ingenuity of it all – the bridges, the tunnels, the rush of cool air as you dive below a mountain.

... simply sit back and let yourself be carried along for the ride.

Travelling by train allows you unrivalled access to these hard-to-reach landscapes – a bridge-eye view of an estuary spilling out to sea; those breathtaking beside-the-water routes, where it feels like you can almost skim your fingers over a lake or the sea.

It's not just epic vistas, either. I'm also here for those mundane, in-between landscapes you so often miss when travelling by car. While SatNav leads drivers along the most direct routes – via motorways, tolls and bypasses – railways drift through suburbs and skim the backs of terraced houses, where you can peep into gardens and see vignettes of early morning routines; it reveals a country distilled through short glimpses into everyday lives.

Crossing borders overland – and witnessing how a landscape changes over vast distances – also blurs the boundaries of place. It begins to unravel the idea of national identity as being rigidly defined. Margins are reimagined, with countries connected by contours, weather, language and gastronomy, rather than by political boundaries.

If you're not in a rush, you might also be tempted to hop off at middle-of-nowhere platforms. On the FEVE railway in northern Spain, I couldn't resist disembarking at the tiny station of Loiba, where a 2km (1¼ mile) walk through eucalyptus woods brought me

Another benefit of rail travel is being able to explore lesser-known back routes ...

to dramatic Praia do Picón, site of the 'most beautiful bench in the world', according to the signs, to watch waves crash into the tilted granite cliffs.

A sense of wonder

I'm sure I'm not the only one who feels enthralled by miniature worlds, from model villages to toy train sets, flea circuses to snowdomes. Dollhouse food particularly gets me – it's those tiny baguettes dusted in flour, minute trays of poached salmon in aspic, neat larders stacked with jars of peaches and preserved lemons. As for model villages, it's partly things like tiny, trimmed privet hedges and mechanical windmills that get me. It's partly, the bewildering shift in time; the fact that it's always a Sunday morning as tiny parishoners gather after a church service, while a minute cricket game is played out for evermore on a manicured village green. And then there's that hall-of-mirrors moment you spot a model village within a model village.

To me, these make-believe worlds within worlds represent a place out of time, one with a promise of stepping outside of our everyday life and into a place with different rules, different ways of being.

You might find this a stretch of imagination, but I feel a similar sense of transcendence when stepping aboard a sleeper train. It's the playful change of scale when you leave the platform – with its vast vaulted ceilings, outsized statues and giant railway clocks – and, via a series of shrinking doors, you enter a world of tiny sinks and secret reading lights, teeny toothbrushes and dinky storage pockets. Everything having a place, everything within reach. For me, this Lilliputian change in scale adds to a sense of being transported to another world. This is a place where wondrous things can happen.

In November 2014, after leaving my job and before launching my independent journal, *Ernest*, I embarked on a trip through Scandinavia. The most memorable – and wondrous – part of my journey was a night on the Norrlandståget sleeper train, a brute of an engine, which ploughs through snow and ice like a real-life *Snowpiercer*, travelling 1,014km (630 miles) from Narvik to Stockholm.

As the train departed, my partner and I settled into our snug berth with its three-up bunks, the view through the curved cabin window a blur of ice-streaked firs and swirling snow. Restless, a couple of hours into the 18-hour journey, we set off along endless slim corridors in search of a buffet car. Much to our surprise, moving between carriages meant sliding open external doors and stepping 'outside' briefly, snow billowing up from the tracks; the soft, muted sound of the train replaced by squealing rails and a smack of cold air.

Eventually, we reached the end of the train. Finding no buffet car, only carriage after carriage of reclining seats and couchettes, we returned to our berth feeling deflated. Several hours later, stretching our legs once again with a short amble down the train, we slid open a door to find a fully decked-out dining car, with plush red velvet booths, polished wooden tables and the scent of

EMBSAY STATION

reindeer stew hanging in the air. Enthralled by this fortuitous and cosy scene appearing out of nowhere, we ordered a bowl of stew and struck up a conversation with an eccentric chap at the bar, chatting late into the evening.

Later that night, my gaze softly focused on the endless indigo twilight outside the window, I realized a new section of the train must have been attached at a previous stop. But in the moment we chose to believe that, much like the Room of Requirement in the *Harry Potter* series, that buffet car had appeared as if by magic just when we needed it most.

The simple delight of train food

As with all types of travel, it can be fun to create your own rituals. For me, street food – specifically, platform food – is a crucial part of what makes rail travel so special. I always aim to allow time to sample local titbits before – and during – a journey to ground myself in each new place.

In my early 20s, I travelled through India by train over many months. I embarked on slow routes through the southern states of Karnataka, Kerala and Tamil Nadu; took a sleeper from Mumbai to Delhi; then travelled west through Rajasthan. Each station brought new sounds, smells, voices and accents – but, more importantly, new flavours.

I loved the way that each time the train pulled into a station, a *chaiwala* (a tea seller, often a young boy) would hop into the carriage bearing a silvery urn of sweet milky tea and a towering stack of small clay cups. Meanwhile, food sellers would start passing delicious street food through the glass-less windows. Each station presented unfamiliar, regional flavours. In Tamil Nadu I tucked into *uttapam*, a spongy pancake topped with colourful veggies. In Karnataka, *masala-dosa* – crispy pancakes stuffed with mustard-spiced boiled potatoes – were the king of bus and train station snacks. But it was in Kerala where I found my dream train breakfast – saucer-shaped rice cakes called *idli*, wrapped in newspaper and served with bright green coconut chutney.

Years later, travelling by train in Japan brought another culinary delight. *Ekiben*, pronounced '*air key ben*', is a special type of bento sold on platform kiosks across Japan. A combination of the Japanese words *eki*, meaning 'station', and *bento*, a Japanese lunch box, these super-fresh meals focus on regional specialities, so you might find salmon roe, crabmeat and rice-stuffed squid in Hokkaido, or impossibly tender Kobe beef in Kansai. Choosing my daily *ekiben* became an essential ritual during my time in Japan.

A brief note on arriving

Arriving by train, especially by sleeper, is a singular experience. Depending on where you're travelling, you may be roused by a polite knock on the door from the steward, or the hacking sound of a hundred men clearing their noses and throats through train windows. A flurry of activity ensues as you hastily pack up your berth, rearrange the bunks into benches and scour your wash kit for some way to make yourself presentable.

Arriving by rail, you're more likely to be right in the heart of things. You might arrive in a thronging city hub, in the midst of domestic travellers and commuters. It's a wholly different experience to being funnelled through an airport arrivals lounge, where every billboard positions you as a 'tourist'. I don't mean that in a derogatory way – we are all tourists when we travel – but having witnessed how the landscape morphs over miles upon miles, heard the way accents and languages evolve, sat beside and even shared food with your fellow travellers, you have already begun to adjust. It's a much less abrupt way to arrive.

If you have time, train stations can also be fascinating places to pause. With their frenzy of travellers, hastily buying a takeout coffee or a quick bite to eat before their train departs, stations might not immediately align with your idea of a slow travel experience. But linger a while; let the people blur around as you take in the rush of sounds, scents and sights. These moments can be enlightening, too. At the very least, it allows you to move on to the next stage of your journey feeling calm and unhurried.

Plus some stations are worth seeking out, whether you're hopping on a train or not. One of my all-time favourites is São Bento Station in Porto, Portugal, with its iconic floor-to-ceiling *azulejo* tiles – 20,000 in total – illuminating Portugal's history of transportation until the 1900s in elegant blue and white. Then there's the Victorian Gothic Chhatrapati Shivaji Terminus in Mumbai, India – an UNESCO

Arriving by rail, you're more likely to be right in the heart of things.

World Heritage Site built to commemorate Queen Victoria's Golden Jubilee in the late 1890s, which unbelievably sees three million travellers pass through each day. With two wings stretching out from an ornate stone dome – a nod to Indian palace architecture – and towers and spires reminiscent of European cathedrals and castles, it's an opulent reminder of the British Raj in India.

Embracing the unexpected

The antithesis of *flygskam* (or 'flight shame'), *tågskryt* is another perfect Swedish word, which literally translates as 'train brag': taking pride in choosing trains over less environmentally friendly means of transport. I have definitely been prone to displays of *tågskryt* over the years.

As well as being more environmentally friendly, travelling by train allows us to open ourselves up to the unknown and transition into the idea of 'journey'. It brings with it a certain acceptance that things won't always go as planned, but if we shift our mindset, we allow our journeys to be guided by curiosity and chance encounters. After all, there are always other routes forward. Sometimes a delayed train is the reason for a memorable encounter, and a missed connection is the catalyst for a wonderful adventure.

圧力確認

What to pack for a cosy night on a sleeper train

Holdall or duffel bag

A big, squashy bag that you can open up fully and rummage around in when it's dark.

Headphones

Download podcasts, audiobooks or playlists for your journey; add a headphone splitter if you're travelling with a friend.

Refillable water bottle

Plus cutlery, to travel lightly without needing single-use plastic.

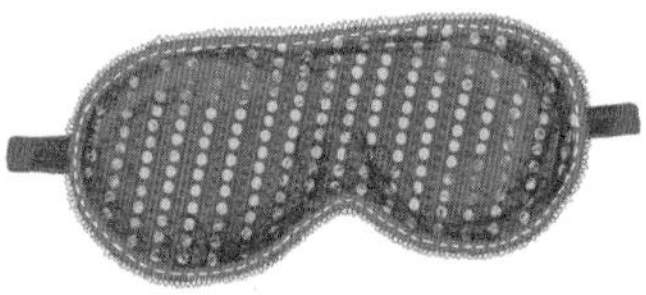

Eye mask

For a good night's rest when sharing a couchette (a four- or six-person carriage with shared facilities) with night owls.

Journal

Travelling by rail sets your mind adrift; document all those meandering thoughts on paper. Not sure where to start? Try giving yourself a prompt or posing yourself a question, then let your thoughts just flow.

A freshen-up kit

Spruce yourself up after 18 hours on a night train with a simple kit comprising toothbrush and paste, biodegradable face wipes, brush, deodorant and whatever else will make you feel ready for the day.

Snacks

Long-distance train travel can be a gloriously self-contained or sociable experience. When sharing a couchette, it's a good idea to bring food to share, to help break the ice with strangers.

Sleeping bag liner

Lightweight to carry, yet adds a clean and cosy layer wherever you're travelling. Natural fibres such as silk or merino offer extra warmth while being breathable in warm weather.

Warm bed socks

Plus comfy, casual clothes that are easy to find in your bag: think drawstring waistbands and a super-soft sweatshirt for overzealous air-conditioning.

Passport

European night trains can pass through several international borders in one trip; keep your passport to hand.

Cards

A wonderful way to push through language barriers and make friends with fellow travellers.

Packing cubes

A traveller's best friend. Keep your kit organised with these handy storage bags. Try organising by need rather than type such as a 'ready for bed' bag, which is much more useful than having all your socks in one place.

On mountain solitude

The Enduring Appeal of Simple Shelters

Chapter six explores the lost art of being alone: how intentional, freely chosen solitude can be a restorative and reflective experience, giving us space to converse with our rich inner worlds or find the time to create.

Wild, mountainous landscapes seem to invite this sort of quiet reflection, where rugged beauty – and a remote and charmingly simple cabin, bothy or shelter – can provide a much-needed interlude in our super-connected lives.

In our age of obsessive, almost fetishistic connectivity, it really can be hard to disconnect. How often are the quiet moments in our lives filled with idle phone scrolling or out-of-hours inbox refreshing? The way we try to stay connected to our work and social lives in this light and potentially unrewarding manner leaves us little space to listen to our inner workings, to play with an idle thought or to envisage potential new futures.

Taking time out, to be alone and in nature, grants us the space to pause. It also gives us time to be attentive, both to our environment and to what is going on within ourselves. It allows us to sit and observe, or move through a landscape that stirs our emotions; then we return to our lives and loved ones, feeling refreshed, grounded and grateful.

Being alone in nature encourages us to be more aware, to notice more. Just as silence heightens the senses, solitude sharpens your awareness. Without the distraction of conversation, we become more sensory aware. We free ourselves to notice the minutest details: the soft play of light, the texture of tree bark and the veining of leaves, the crunch of our boots on the forest floor. The more we notice, the more we appreciate the value of the environment, and our connection with it.

There is even scientific evidence to suggest that spending time in nature can restore cognitive function. In Dr David Strayer's 2017 Ted talk 'Restore Your Brain with Nature', the psychology professor at the University of Utah explains how multi-tasking and our near-constant use of technology, can overuse the pre-frontal cortex of the brain, causing fatigue.

This is also the part of our brains that is responsible for decision-making, problem solving and critical thinking. Spending time in the wild, especially alone when we are freed from conversation and social dynamics, can restore these faculties, improving short-term memory, creativity and problem solving as well as lowering stress levels and encouraging feelings of wellbeing.

Just as silence heightens the senses, solitude sharpens your awareness.

Intentional solitude is a gift to ourselves. It is an opportunity to carve out the space we need: to reflect on our lives and to work through anything that is troubling us; to grieve, to adjust, to accept. It brings us back to our truest selves, without getting caught up in how others perceive us or what is expected of us. It gives us space to accept who we are and where we are at, without rushing to address or resolve our problems. It allows us to simply be. This, in turn, fosters appreciation, and helps us to be more authentic in our connection with others when we return.

The contradictions of being alone

Is it easy to be alone? Well, in principle, yes. In reality, it can feel like one of the most challenging things you can do. How can something so basic, so necessary, feel so confronting?

For one thing, people often have polarizing views on spending time alone; we either crave it or avoid it at all costs. It is often judged and stigmatized; other people may even pity or feel suspicious of those who elect to spend time by themselves, particularly in 'social' public places such as restaurants.

Even for those of us who value it, it can still feel as unnerving as it is inviting. Spending time by yourself, especially when travelling and staying elsewhere, comes with a simultaneous feeling of apprehension and curiosity. When we are alone, we cannot escape ourselves – what might we encounter in these quiet moments?

It is helpful to remember that intentional, freely chosen solitude is not the same as loneliness. In her book, *How to Be Alone*, Sara Maitland addresses some of these reservations, going on to explain that underlying our anxiety, there are fundamental contradictions around attitudes to solitude that need to be unpicked.

We live in a world that values high self-esteem, autonomy, individuality, creativity and personal growth above all else, yet we rarely take the time to get better acquainted with this one-off, independent and imaginative person. Even as someone who values solitude and tries to make space for it in my life, I found this such a startling and insightful idea. Because it's true; how can we know our minds, if we don't take time to get to know (and accept) ourselves?

Even as someone who values solitude and tries to make space for it in my life, I found this such a startling and insightful statement. Because it's true; we are taught to value autonomy, individuality, creativity and personal growth above all else, yet we rarely take the time to get better acquainted with this one-off, independent and imaginative person. How can we know our minds, if we don't take time to get to know (and accept) ourselves?

Seeking refuge in wild mountainscapes

While you don't have to go somewhere wild to spend time by yourself, mountains and untamed wilderness does carry a certain allure.

Perhaps we are inspired by the rich tradition in memoir – writers and poets who have retreated to wild places and written about their experiences in honest, reflective and enticing detail.

Memoirs of note include *Walden*, in which 28-year-old Henry David Thoreau retreats to a self-built cabin in the woods in Massachusetts, meditating on (among other things) the nature of solitude and loneliness. *The Living Mountain*, a masterpiece of nature writing in which Nan Shepherd describes her journeys into Scotland's Cairngorms mountains, her imaginative relationship with the wild world around us and reflections of what we love and value in the world. In *Wild*, Cheryl Strayed embarks, age 26, on a 4,286-km (2,663-mile) journey between the west coast of Mexico and Canada on the Pacific Crest Trail in the wake of her mother's death and the breakdown of her marriage. And then there's America's Beat Generation poets and writers who spent time in remote fire lookout cabins in the Pacific Northwest's mountainous North Cascades in the 1950s such as Philip Whalen who wrote of it in 'Sourdough Mountain Lookout', and Jack Kerouac who spent 63 days on Desolation Peak in the summer of 1956.

I have often pondered what it is about mountains that carry this enticing appeal. From hillforts to mountain-top monasteries, people have always sought refuge in high places. They represent safety and sanctuary.

There is also something about the expansiveness of a mountain panorama that opens the mind to new possibilities. Being able to see into the far distance offers perspective, suggesting potential new futures. Seeing the landscape unfold before you over great distances affords metaphorical perspective; it helps us to imagine how we can move beyond our horizons and grants us freedom to change our situations.

Perhaps there is something in the geology, too. Mountain landscapes are the oldest, most inert and steady places we could imagine. There is something particularly magical in finding traces of seabed or sea creatures on summits; this is old land, which bestows a sense of permanence. We feel small within these landscapes, and time loses relevance. You can have a startling realization of your own impermanence and a sense of perspective about your everyday cares.

Mountains are also mostly still landscapes, a place where we can pause our racing minds. You are far less likely to see other people. This deep silence allows you to listen to your inner thoughts; I find that it invites kindness and gives space to find acceptance. Here, you can recapture a part of yourself that has laid dormant or been suppressed in place of career ambitions.

Mountains often form dividing boundary lines between nations, territories or countries.

Intentional solitude is a gift to ourselves. It is an opportunity to carve out the space we need ...

There's something in this, which invites us to contemplate our life choices and envisage new chapters. One of my most treasured places to walk, which naturally helps me to enter into this frame of mind, is the Black Mountains, a series of parallel ridges that form the bulky western wall of Wales.

This is borderland; walking along the spine of Hatterrall Ridge, where wild ponies graze amid spiky gorse and nodding ferns, you can place one foot in Wales and the other in England. To the east, you look out over the Marches, an undulating pastoral vision of fields and forest; a silver slither of water, the Bristol Channel, glints in the far distance. To the West, the buff contours of the Brecon Beacons rise up towards the dark table-top online of Pen-y-Fan.

I cannot count the number of times I have trodden these paths, and others like them, and deliberated between the differing directions I could take. Similarly, just as boundaries can help you to imagine a new chapter; paths can represent metaphorical ways forward, a catalyst for a new direction in life.

Solitude for the uninitiated

There is no one size fits all when it comes to solitude. The duration doesn't matter; it is more about shifting into a new mindset. So treat every solo expedition, however small, as practice. Push your comfort level over time; you might find that each time you do it, you will gain more from the experience.

Choosing to spend time alone in nature does not necessarily mean being still. While some people choose to reflect quietly and open themselves up for inner inspection through stillness in nature, others prefer to move, to put themselves through physical endurance in order to meet with themselves. Walking, swimming, cycling and running are all ways of spending time alone. While travelling alone, it is important to set your own pace and your own agenda. Leave space to notice your thoughts and be open to what you might discover.

If you prefer, you can still find solitude in the comfort of company. You can build pockets of solitude into communal trips, or walk silently with a companion, giving each other the chance to drift in thought.

Writing for *Ernest*, outdoor therapist Ruth Allen, explains: 'Solitude doesn't have to mean permanent retreat, or rejection of the people we share our lives with. Instead, practising solitude allows you to go back to that world refreshed and able to engage more wholeheartedly, having had time out from it. We take less for granted and our relationships feel more authentic. Solitude is a practice and a mindset, and it enriches the company we keep – it allows us to discover our true, best and most difficult selves, and how we may come to fit all of that harmoniously within our shared humanity.'

The enduring appeal of basic shelters

Getting away from it all and spending time in a simple hideaway has an enduring appeal – from writer's cabins to alpine huts and Scottish

bothies. In our super-connected, often cluttered lives, the idea of a simple cabin, nestled within the landscape as if it has always been there, holds a distinct charm; a place for our restless minds to settle.

The minimal nature of these spaces seems to somehow promise clarity. How often have I sought this, at times when life and deadlines became overwhelming? A modest, homely place to simply write, with no signal or distractions; a place to detangle my thoughts, to think clearly.

Their bare-bones simplicity also evokes the idea of having 'just enough'. It represents a yearning for a simple, more 'authentic' life. And there is that tantalizing prospect: could I sell all my stuff and actually live here? Even looking at woodsy cabins can feel calming, as the popularity of websites and books such as *Cabinporn* can attest.

Mountain bothies

One of the most basic examples of a simple shelter in wild landscapes is the mountain bothy. Deriving from the Gaelic *bothan* (from the Old Irish *both*) meaning 'hut', bothies once provided rough and ready accommodation for farm workers, shepherds and ghillies (attendants on a hunt or expedition). Built in the most remote and uninhabited parts of Scotland, northern England and Wales, these basic stone structures now provide shelter for hikers and climbers, offering protection from the elements as well as safety and warmth within an imposing landscape.

The Mountain Bothies Association (MBA) looks after 85 bothies in Scotland, 12 in England and 9 in Wales, breathing new life into these formerly dilapidated shelters. Found in remote locations, often several hours' walk from the nearest road, these open shelters are left unlocked for travellers in need of four walls and a roof; a place to shelter when caught out in a storm.

If you think the idea of sleeping out in the wild, in a ramshackle shelter hundreds of years old, sounds romantic, think again. These 'stone tents' have no running water or electricity. Some have compost loos, while others provide a shovel beside the door. Don't expect comfy furniture or beds, either. Usually they have an open fire for drying your boots, hooks for hanging wet clothes, perhaps a table and a couple of rickety chairs and a guestbook with notes dating back decades. It is a touch of bare-bones comfort in an otherwise inhospitable landscape.

There are no formal rules, but visitors are requested to follow the 'Bothy Code', loose common-sense etiquette that ensures the bothies are left in good shape. The code talks of respect, of welcoming and being considerate to others. Although you will often have a bothy to yourself, these are open shelters, available to all and there is absolutely no recognized concept of 'first come, first served'. The ethos is that 'there is always room for one more'.

Bothies are a 'celebration of a simple existence in the wild', Rich Baldwin wrote for *Ernest*, describing how window-rattling stormy nights gave way to the glow of dawn sunlight; how he disturbed a herd of deer with the noise of the latch as he stepped out into the cold mountain air. Solitude isn't guaranteed. Often a wisp of smoke is a telltale sign that you will have company for the night. But other times you will lift the latch to find the entire place to yourself.

Once closely guarded secrets, many of these simple shelters are now listed on the MBA's online map and compiled in books such as

The Scottish Bothy Bible and *Scottish Bothy Walks*. They are free to use, maintained by dedicated, hardy volunteers.

Similar utilitarian structures can be found around the world from Nordic and alpine countries to the USA, Canada and New Zealand. Providing primitive shelter for climbers and mountaineers, these wilderness (or backcountry) huts often teeter on the edge of rocky pinnacles or deep in the forest, in the midst of sublime natural landscapes.

In the German Alps, there are *biwakschachtels* ('bivouac boxes'). Adirondack lean-tos developed in the Adirondack Mountains of Upstate New York and now seen in other US national and state parks, are three-sided log camping platforms. In the Great Smoky Mountains National Park straddling North Carolina and Tennessee, backcountry huts offer through hikers on the Appalachian Trail a simple space to rest their aching legs.

Solitude isn't guaranteed. Often a wisp of smoke is a telltale sign that you will have company for the night.

Arguably the wildest way to sleep out in the open is to use a *boofen* (pronounced 'bo-fen'), an even simpler, natural shelter used by climbers in the deeply forested and sculptural Elbe Sandstone Mountains of German-speaking Saxon Switzerland. Deriving from the colloquial German word for deep sleep, 'pofen', the *boofen* dates to the beginning of the twentieth century. Not actually a hand-built shelter, these 58 designated areas will likely be a cave or an overhang in the sandstone rock.

Rather than roughing it, a stay here is all about taking things slowly ... and returning to nature.

A cosy or creative retreat

Of course, you don't need to retreat to such spartan lodgings in search of solitude. Across Scotland (and around the world), bothies are having a glow up. Places like Inverlonan – three bothies named *Uisge* (pronounced 'oosh-ka'), *Beatha* ('bay-ah') and *Sitheil* ('she-eel') nestling between ancient oaks and overlooking Loch Nell near Oban – are reimagining the bothy experience, offering 'rough luxury, seclusion and the chance to disconnect from the day-to-day'.

The cabins are only accessible by boat, foot or buggy, and have outdoor wood-fired pizza ovens, homely Scottish textiles and cosy woodburners. Provisions are delivered to the door, and a lochside sauna is nearby. Rather than roughing it, a stay here is all about taking things slowly, getting back to the basics and returning to nature.

Another initiative, independent charitable organization The Bothy Project provides creative residences in small-scale, off-grid creative spaces to 'explore creativity, landscape and living simply'. Artists who have stayed in one of their three bothies describe how being away from phone signal and wifi changed their mindset. They talk about time becoming different; how days revolve around daily walks, chopping wood, filling water bottles and retreating back into the warmth of the cabin with enough sunlight to read books.

'It might seem absurd to think we need to completely remove ourselves from ordinary life to see our work clearly, but for me, this was the case,' wrote Grace Denton, who took a solo residency in Sweeney's Bothy, on the Isle of Eigg. 'The cloud-like distraction of the internet, of daily demands, of conflicting things we feel we "should" be doing as artists, can make it impossible to focus on the art itself.'

Although we've focused on the appeal of remote mountain landscapes, freely chosen solitude isn't just for wild and faraway places. In the conclusion, we explore ways to seek out this solitude closer to home; how creating opportunities to press pause in our everyday lives can help us to foster a deep sense of belonging and spending a little less of your time 'doing' and little more simply 'being'. But first, it's time to explore slow travel with a wholly different environment ...

What to pack for a night in a bothy

Head torch

For cooking in the twilight, late-night reading and nocturnal 'toilet' trips. Don't forget spare batteries.

A bothy guide

Gone are the days when bothy locations were kept hush-hush, passed between seasoned hikers by word of mouth. Today, books such as The Scottish Bothy Bible *and The Mountain Bothies Association website provide detailed directions and insights into these special places.*

Simple food

Plan for basic dishes to cook up in one pan, such as porridge, pasta or dehydrated food. There is often a Highland stream nearby, with water you can boil to cook with. Always boil before drinking.

Map and compass

Weather conditions can deteriorate quickly in the Scottish Highlands, so knowing how to use a compass is crucial when a lack of visibility means you can no longer read the landscape. Consider taking a navigation course before going to more remote locations.

Firewood and firelighters

Most bothies have a fireplace, but you will need to bring your own firewood and kindling. If there is leftover wood, always replace what you use and leave dry kindling for those who come after you.

Warm sleeping bag and mat

Pack the warmest sleeping bag you can carry comfortably, plus a silk or merino liner for an extra 5°C of snugness. While most bothies have sleeping platforms (wooden shelves raised off the floor), you may be sleeping on the floor, so a comfy sleeping mat is also a must.

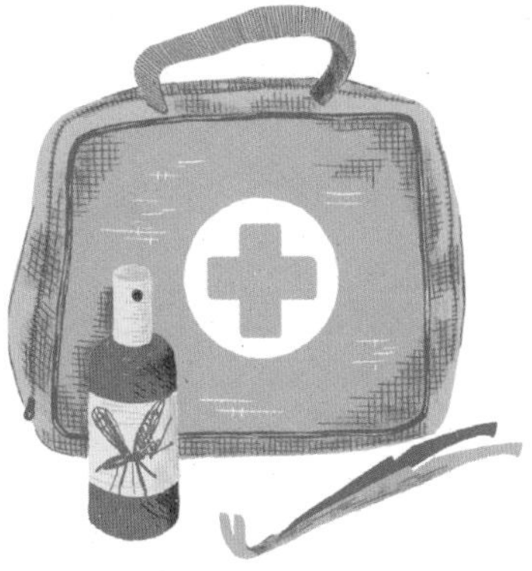

Hiking first aid kit

In the Scottish summer, if the ticks don't get you, the midges will. So as well as the usual blister plasters, dressings and antiseptics, pack some natural midge spray and tick tweezers.

Camping stove

A lightweight camping cook set, where the stove, pans and plates (even forks) stack inside each other, will save valuable space in your backpack. .

Whisky

Chances are, you won't have the bothy to yourself. So why not sit around a roaring fire, sharing a 'wee dram' of something warming, as you share tales from the trail?

Ear plugs and eye mask

Expect to sleep in close quarters with strangers; earplugs make sure you're not disturbed by snoring. Bothies also rarely have curtains, so an eye mask is a must.

On drifting

Urban Landscapes

In stark contrast to the previous chapter, we should not overlook the buzzing, thriving, frenetic energy that many of us love about city travel. Cities can be a cultural microcosm, a distilled and intoxicating concoction of a country's heritage, architecture and gastronomy. A 24- or 48-hour trip can be a tempting option for the time poor, who want to get the most out of every trip.

Whistlestop city breaks, however, can also be expensive, intense and downright exhausting. With a short duration, long list of must-sees and hyped expectations, they could be a typical recipe for travel fatigue.

Also known as travellers' burnout, travel fatigue more often affects long-term travellers who spend weeks and months on high 'alert' while travelling, manifesting as apathy, weariness and a deep sense of disengagement. However, the hectic schedule, late nights and self-imposed pressure to see and do everything a city has to offer that often accompanies a quick city break can certainly take its toll and bring on a case of the wearies.

To travel 'slowly' within a dynamic city vibe may feel like a contradiction in terms but adopting a more intentional mindset while exploring cities can add so much depth to your experience – leaving you feeling energized rather than burnt out.

The first step to travelling more intentionally is to allow ourselves more time. If you can, why not take a week to explore a city and the surrounding area? Exploring one place well gives us an opportunity to immerse ourselves in the soul of a city, getting under its skin and allowing us to connect more deeply, see more and appreciate more.

Another way to open the door to more authentic experiences is to seek out smaller, off-beat and often overlooked destinations – otherwise known as the tourism 'B-list'. This not only counters the problem of overtourism in more popular destinations – an issue where 'too many' people descend on a destination, causing crowding, damaging fragile natural or historic environments and pushing up the cost of living for local residents – it also encourages us to carve our own paths and strive for more unique experiences.

In the UK, this might mean skipping a trip to 'Shakespeare country' in Stratford-upon-Avon and

The first step to travelling more intentionally is to allow ourselves more time.

instead exploring the half-timbered houses and historic markets of Shrewsbury or Hereford; or giving Brighton a miss in favour of seaside Margate's independent shops and eccentric art scene. In Europe, you might choose to forego Stockholm and instead ferry hop between Helsinki in Finland and Tallinn in Estonia for icy Baltic dips and harbourside fish feasts followed by one of the most superbly preserved medieval cities in Europe. Swap Grenada for the Andalusian city of Córdoba; Prague for Brno; Marseille for Toulouse. You get the idea.

If you have your heart set on a popular destination, consider booking during the low or shoulder season. Not only might this facilitate an experience that feels more rewarding for you, you will also be supporting local businesses that rely on visitors all the year round.

Once you arrive at your destination, you can then plot a course for lesser-known sights. Instead of hunting down the top 10 places to visit, channel your curiosity by seeking out overlooked neighbourhoods and suburbs, or by venturing down the city's back roads.

Personally, I am a big fan of bypassing busy streets and taking more circuitous routes. When I lived in Brighton, I would always take an opportunity to detour down its many 'twittens' – an old Sussex dialect word describing a narrow passageway between buildings (growing up in Lancashire, we called them 'ginnels' or 'snickets'). It was once said that you could journey from one side of the town to the other using these alleyways.

Venturing down these hidden streets, I not only evaded slow-moving day trippers in the city's famous Lanes, I also discovered beautiful flint-fronted cottages and tiny oases behind wrought-iron fences; I brushed leaves to reveal old shop floor mosaics beneath my feet and stumbled upon the historic 'border' between Brighton and its neighbour, Hove.

Keep it local

So many of the slow travel principles we discuss throughout this book can apply to city travel. Meeting local residents is still one of the best ways to immerse ourselves in a destination, and staying with a local host isn't just reserved for remote locations. Couch surfing and private house or flat rentals (the 'old fashioned' type of place, where you get to know your host rather than pristine B&Bs with key safes) afford opportunities for you to get to know someone who lives in the city, to ask for their recommendations and to see the streets through their eyes. Spend time getting to know your host, hearing their homegrown recommendations; they will often have far more insight than what a guidebook or online article can offer.

You can also keep it local through the food you eat. Local ingredients and dishes tell us stories about how people live in a city and the surrounding countryside. Take the opportunity to delve into a city's food culture by buying ingredients from local markets, talking to people selling and preparing local food, and appreciating

FARR'S LANE

the rhythms of local life. Even in a busy city, you can still pick up bread from a neighbourhood bakery, browse local fruit and veg markets and sit at the bar of a local wine merchant or taproom, finding out the stories behind local tipples.

The upshot of many of these slow travel intentions is that you often also save money. Eating locally, staying with a local host, exploring on foot and choosing less popular city destinations are all ways to cut down on costs.

Just as with slow travel in more remote locations, however you spend your time it pays not to rush. Remember the mantra 'there is always another trip'. One way to do this is to explore on foot, and to pay attention to your pace. Purposefully slowing down to an amble gives you time to observe the details that bring cities to life.

Be intentional about spending your days at a relaxed pace, and deliberately linger. Spend a whole day browsing bookshops; explore one museum or art gallery thoroughly rather than rushing between two or three; or take time out to sit outside a cafe and simply observe.

The simple joy of people watching

Scratching away in a sketchbook or journal not only offers a socially acceptable reason to be on your own in public, it also allows you to people watch to your heart's content. Documenting your observations with a pen and paper also sharpens your eye and helps you to notice rich, new details. It teaches us to see the world more clearly and gives us a deeper feeling of presence in that moment.

As Victorian art critic John Ruskin noted in the 1800s, sketching helps us see the world with renewed wonder and curiosity. In an essay on the psychology of drawing, he gives the example of two people walking down a green lane. While

Take the opportunity to delve into a city's food culture by buying ingredients from local markets ...

one notes that the trees are green and the sun shines with a cheerful effect, the sketcher's eyes penetrate the minutiae of beauty. He observes the hundred varied colours of gnarled wood, 'the jewel brightness of the emerald moss', and 'how the showery and subdivided sunshine comes sprinkled down among the gleaming leaves overhead'.

A few years ago, writing an article for *The Simple Things*, I challenged myself to sketch daily for a fortnight and it helped me notice a whole new side to my city. I had walked over Pero's Bridge in Bristol's harbour tens of times, but when I decided to sit down and sketch it, it suddenly felt unfamiliar. My focus shifted from the trudge of commuters and the fluorescent blur of cyclists to the smallest detail. I saw greenery pushing through the harbour wall and how the bridge's counterweight 'horns' curved at completely different angles. I observed how the greyish-green water created eddies below while the arrival of the local ferry left a gaggle of smaller boats to creak and bob in its wake.

Sketching gave me a reason to tune in to my surroundings, and find wonder in the familiar, and to see the world with renewed curiosity. For a start, I noticed that the city's weathervanes were not cockerels but ships! Over time, I built up a distinctive and very personal document of a place. I came to realize that while taking photos allows us to capture a moment, drawing encourages us to pull out symbolism and meaning; to observe in a more involved way; to notice light, texture, movement and nuance.

By drawing, we don't simply recreate an image of a scene, you capture its essence. I would go so far as to say, it also changes how you see. Beyond helping you notice details, drawing gives you a subjective filter through which to see the world. Documenting this on paper helps you to realize what you find beautiful and, in essence, to acknowledge what is important to you.

Urban navigation

'Not to find one's way in a city may well be uninteresting and banal. It requires ignorance, nothing more,' wrote the twentieth-century philosopher-essayist Walter Benjamin. 'But to lose oneself in a city – as one loses oneself in a forest – that calls for quite a different schooling.'

I first discovered this wonderful quote in *A Field Guide to Getting Lost* by Rebecca Solnit. For Benjamin, writing in the 1920s and 1930s, to be lost was to be truly present; to drift through one's environment, and voluntarily surrender and immerse oneself in the city.

In his writing, Benjamin draws on the character of the urban 'flâneur', a French noun referring to a 'stroller', 'an idler' or an 'urban explorer'. The word derives from the Old Norse verb *flana*, meaning 'to wander with no purpose'. It is suggestive of someone who walks without purpose while acutely observing urban life. They are a spectator and an investigator, drifting in the ebb and flow of a crowded city. But how do we channel this carefree and idle way of travelling in our city explorations, today?

One way to do this might be to disrupt how we explore a city; to find new ways of navigating even familiar places so that we can rekindle our sense of curiosity.

There are many ways we can bring this practice into our urban explorations. One of the easiest steps is to experience the city on foot. Walking without distraction can help us get into a flow state, meaning that we are fully immersed in what we are doing. You will probably have experienced this psychological state before – perhaps through meditation, or a day-to-day task or creative piece of work that completely absorbs your attention. It's that feeling of being 'in the zone', when time seems to slow down and you are carried forward with an effortless momentum.

While that might sound tricky within a city, there are plenty of ways to help 'lose yourself'. Laying out a map of a new city, I often seek out its waterways – canal towpaths, riverside walkways or harbours. One of the benefits of walking beside canals, for instance, is that they are easy to navigate. Even in buzzing cities like London, Amsterdam or Paris, you can plan a route from A to B beside a canal and feel confident you're not going to physically lose your way. With the directions taken care of, you are free to amble and to let your mind drift.

Another way to get into a flow is to focus on a new way of navigating. I once went for a walk with 'natural navigator' Tristan Gooley, who shared invaluable insights on navigating in urban environments. Natural navigation is the rare art of finding your way by observing natural clues, without using a map, compass or SatNav. It relies on simple skills such as awareness and deduction, getting your bearings through intuition and insight.

RIMOWA
MICHAEL KORS
ORCHARD LINK

DHC
Google Home
TSUTAYA

109MEN'S
私をリフトする。
RF × 超音波
ZARA
109MEN'S

Although it's a practice more often used in wilder environments, you can use many of the techniques in urban spaces, and Tristan has come up with many tricks and tips to help people navigate cities.

One thing he suggests is to note the flow of people through a city. In the morning, a steady stream of people will be moving away from train or underground stations, while in the late afternoon you can follow this flow of people to find these places. Christian churches usually align west-east, with the altar at the eastern end (gravestones are also aligned west-east), which can be useful for finding your bearings.

You can also orient yourself by reading weathering on buildings. Algae grows on the shaded, northern side of structures, for instance. Prevailing winds also carry rain and pollution, which weathers buildings over time. In the UK, the wind often

How do we channel this carefree and idle way of travelling in our city explorations, today?

comes from the southwest, so you can find your way by noticing where the stone looks grubbier.

Finding wildness in the city

Urban environments have a different resonance to wilder places: a background hum of traffic, building sites, human voices and air-conditioning units. Finding quieter, green (and blue) spaces presents an opportunity to pause and to check in with ourselves; to turn down the volume on human noise and to tune in to bird calls, the wind through leaves, or the sound of moving water instead. Once you tune into more natural sounds, your other senses might also attune.

Public parks, cemeteries and canal towpaths: these places might feel mundane and unremarkable compared with the remote mountainscapes of the previous chapter. However, these are all places where you can pay attention to what's around you and feel present. Carving out time to visit these green oases will help you slow down and ground yourself within a city.

There are many notable city parks around the world, which form an integral part of everyday life for citizens; places to rest, play and gather away from offices and busy streets. Measuring 5km by 1.5km (3 miles by 1 mile), with an astounding 78km (48 miles) of footpaths, Munich's Englischer Garten (English Garden) in Germany is one of the largest inner-city parks in the world. A green

corridor through the heart of the city, this is where residents kick back with some tai chi and yoga, stretch slacklines between trees, surf in the brisk Eisbach (German for 'ice brook'), unwind in open-air biergärtens and sunbathe in the nip. To avoid the livelier southern half of the park, take a metro to Munchener Freiheit, then head north once you enter the park with its wild grassy meadows and seasonal flocks of sheep.

Then there's San Francisco, which has an incredible 220 parks and urban green spaces, making it one of the greenest cities in the world. This includes Crissy Field, a military airstrip transformed into a waterfront nature reserve where herons and egrets forage on the reclaimed tidal marsh and 1¼-sq-km (312-acre) McLaren Park where miles of trails wind through forest, grasslands and wetlands. The city also has over 40 'pocket parks': small, community-driven green spaces with vibrant murals, living plant walls and mosaic statues.

Of course, urban green spaces aren't always outside; many cities offer numerous hidden botanical spaces indoors. The Barbican Conservatory in London – the second biggest glass conservatory in London, after Kew Gardens – houses 2,000 species of tropical plants and trees, and is free to visit two days per week. It is set within the wider surrounds of the Barbican Estate, a complex of uncompromising Brutalist architecture softened by greenery. While in Madrid, Spain, Atocha train station boasts a 43,000-square-foot (nearly 4,000-square-metre) botanical garden replete with 7,000 tropical plants. Growing high into the station's vast atrium are: Polynesian breadfruit and coconut trees; Cuban mahogany; Central American cacao plants; even a traveller's tree from Madagascar. Until recently, the lily-strewn ponds were home to North and South American freshwater turtles, abandoned pets rescued from Madrid's waterways.

City cemeteries & skygardens

City cemeteries call to slow travellers, drawn by their quiet, respectful ambience, access to green space and urban wildlife. These are places to pause and to reflect, often found right in the heart of lively neighbourhoods.

In some cities, cemeteries have become so popular they have become hybrid city parks. In Copenhagen's culturally diverse and creative Nørrebro district, Assistens Cemetery is a green oasis where local residents sunbathe and picnic on the lawns, expressing true Danish laidbackness, while visitors seek out the graves of notable Danes such as fairy tale author Hans Christian Andersen, physicist Niels Bohr and existentialist philosopher and poet Søren Kierkegaard.

They are also places where the often-rich wildlife of our cities can roam freely. If you're visiting London, the Magnificent Seven – seven cemeteries established on the 'outskirts' of London in the nineteenth century, which have since been enveloped by the sprawling capital – are definitely worth seeking out. They range from the wild and ramshackle – graves hidden by undergrowth, overrun by blackberry brambles or weathered to the point of illegibility – to the stately, with manicured wildflower meadows and vast catacombs. They also bring you close to the capital's rich urban wildlife: parakeets screech overhead in blurs of vibrant green, tawny owls hoot from tree hollows and great spotted woodpeckers drum like creaky barn doors.

Another of the wonderful things about cemeteries is that they often offer a chance to spend time among trees, sometimes even ancient woodland, right in the heart of bustling cities. Research has shown this is crucial not only for the health of our urban wildlife, but for its human inhabitants, too.

In her book *Losing Eden*, Lucy Jones examines research done in Japan, where

shinrin-yoku (or forest bathing) has been formally enshrined since the 1980s. A team of scientists there investigated why being in woodland reduced stress levels considerably. Qing Li, from the Nippon Medical School, discovered that being in a forest for two hours boosted the immune system by increasing the number of natural killer (NK) cells, possibly through phytonicides – chemicals released by trees and plants in woodlands. Asian tree species such as cypress and cedar emit phytonicides, but so do native British and European trees such as oak, birch and beech.

Thankfully, developers and placemakers are beginning to incorporate trees in urban design, often backed by immense community support. One of the most notable, Seoul Skygarden (its full name is the Seoullo 7017 Skygarden), revived a disused 1970s overpass with a 'library' of 24,000 plants, indigenous species ordered according to the Korean alphabet. This 983m- (3,225ft-) long park whips pedestrians high above the traffic and trainlines, connecting districts that have been separated by roads and railway tracks. An inner-city arboretum, with seasonal displays of spring cherry blossom, edible berries in summer, autumn maples and evergreen conifers in winter, the garden invites residents and visitors to slow down and sit for a while among the trees, right in the heart of the capital.

With its first phase opening in 2009, The High Line in New York City is perhaps the most inspiring and established greenway of its kind. What began as an elevated, derelict freight railway, is now a continuous 2.3-km- (nearly 1½ mile-) long linear park featuring 640 species of plants and trees, with planting inspired by the self-seeded landscape that grew wild for 25 years after the trains stopped running. Here you can sit or walk, enveloped within greenery, two stories above the New York streets. Open meadows with prairie-like grasses run into miniature forests of birch and dogwood, amid old railway tracks and sleepers; vines cascade over the railings and a canopy flyover brings pedestrians face to face with the trees: bigleaf magnolia and aromatic sassafras.

Developers and placemakers are beginning to incorporate trees in urban design, often backed by immense community support.

Tools to help you slow down in the city

Film camera

Documenting your trip with an analogue film camera can be a mindful experience; it encourages you to take fewer photos and trust in the moment, to look at a scene in more detail and be thoughtful about how you capture the details.

Reusable coffee cup

Pack a reusable cup to flit from coffee shop to cafe, or take your hot brew to an urban park, without depending on disposables. Collapsible silicone styles, which fit neatly into a waist pack or pocket, and leak-proof lids, might be particularly appealing to an urban traveller.

Pocket binoculars

It's incredible what you can see when you look up in a city: swifts swooping into the eaves of churches, starlings in murmeration over railway bridges, even a peregrine diving for prey. Keep a compact pair of binoculars to hand so you can tune into urban birdlife.

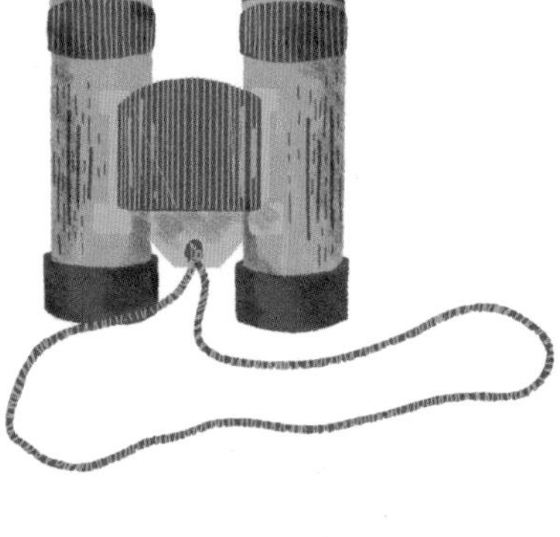

Comfy shoes

An urban flâneur drifts through the city, wandering without purpose and simply observing urban life. And for that they need comfy shoes, which are also smart enough to 'drift' into an upmarket restaurant, if the fancy takes you.

Sketchbook

Choose a slim A5 sketchbook, filled with recycled, non-bleached paper, which can easily slip into your bag. Add a fine-liner pen; there are no mistakes with sketching so no need to rub out pencil lines. .

Waist bag

A versatile, surprisingly roomy bag, which encourages you to travel lightly and keeps your valuables safe in crowded streets. Wear it around your waist or sling it over your shoulder.

Alternative maps

Keep an eye out for illustrated maps that draw out the eccentric or green details of a city, from urban nature and city lidos to maps that focus on a city's literary history or hidden streets.

Waterproof

A lightweight, long-line jacket or poncho, to keep exploring no matter what the weather. Look for a good waterproof rating, breathability and taped seams.

Tote bag

Roll up a canvas tote bag and pop it in a rucksack pocket; if you stumble upon a neighbourhood market, you can pick up ingredients.

VOUCHERS
AVAILABLE

Conclusion

Travel is often something we feel we need to go away to do, which has an allocated time before we return to our 'normal lives'. But what if we were to bring the mindset of slow travel into our everyday lives? Our final part of the book is all about bringing everything we learn while travelling back home, so that we can live more mindfully and embrace the slow adventures on our doorsteps.

The idea of embracing a slow travel mindset closer to home is perhaps even more pertinent since COVID brought our lives to a standstill, altering not only how we travel but arguably shifting our outlook on many elements of our lives for good.

For many of us, lockdowns were enforced pauses, which not only gave us time to reflect on what we need to feel safe and connected, but which also made us focus on what was close to home and immediately available for our health and wellbeing. In many ways, we haven't – in fact, we can't – go back to how things were before.

Another important consequence of the pandemic was to unlink the association between adventure and far-flung destinations. After all, we don't need to travel to another country to experience nature; we don't need to stay in a cabin in the woods to take time to ourselves; we don't need to volunteer abroad to give back and feel connected.

The past few years has arguably also shifted the focus towards not only local travel but also to our inward journeys. The discomfort we felt at not being able to be productive; the shedding of identities and roles; the way we slowly became more comfortable with doing less and being slow. There was a kernel of wisdom within these experiences which many of us have kept even when the pace of our working and home lives picked up once more.

Finding time for slowness in your everyday life, however, can be challenging. It can feel much harder to embrace these values in the same way as when we travel further afield. Back home, we are much more likely to spend time indoors, for instance. When we do spend time outside, we often find ourselves caught up with tasks and commitments. It can feel much harder to immerse ourselves within a landscape or culture, to allow our journeys to be guided by curiosity and to embrace spontaneity.

Shifting down a gear or two and giving ourselves time to nurture our connection with local environments, both urban and remote, however, can be genuinely rewarding. It might not even take as much time or effort as you imagine. Embracing a slow travel mindset in your everyday life can be as simple as choosing not to take the bus or train to work but instead to seek out green pathways through your city. Establishing routines and rituals that help you to find emotional stillness in exhilarating urban environments, seeking out the green amid the grey, and finding new ways to navigate familiar places, are all pathways to channeling your curiosity to find new meaning in the day-to-day.

Reflections

One way to bring what you learn through slow travel back into your life is to reflect on how you spend your time and what you truly appreciate when travelling, then weave this into your everyday life. Perhaps it's shopping for ingredients in a local market and chatting to vendors about the provenance of the food, then working out the small changes you can make back home to live more sustainability and with great connection. Or perhaps it's leaving your comfort zone and realizing that familiar landscapes can still offer unknowns and challenges; knowing you can work on expanding your boundaries, rather than travelling further afield.

Getting involved with local groups and activities can help foster a sense of belonging. After all, if you would consider volunteering abroad, why not do it at home? Take part in a beach clean; join a local food co-op or permaculture project; volunteer at your local allotment or food bank. Be open to conversations and connections the same way you would while travelling.

On belonging

Slow travel encourages us to reconnect with our sense of place. Bringing these slow travel practices into our everyday lives is all about forging new connections, channeling our innate curiosity and fostering a sense of belonging.

Belonging is important. Our emotional ties to place can be summed up by the concept of topophilia. The term is taken from the Greek *topos*, meaning 'place', and *-philia*, meaning 'love of', literally means 'the love of place'. The concept has been reinvented by several writers, philosophers and geographers over the years, but effectively explains our emotional ties to place. Poet W.H. Auden used the term to explain a strong sense of place relating to a sense of cultural history, while human geographer Yi-Fu Tuan defined it as 'the affective bond between people and place or setting', to mean the innate bond between people and place.

It can be summed up as a fondness for home or familiar places, or our bond to our local area, through attention and presence; going back to the same places time and time again. Topophilia plays out through our outdoor experience, whether that's hiking, exploring historic towns, taking time to sit in the sunshine or taking care of your garden.

To foster a sense of belonging, we can ask ourselves: how can we feel rooted in where we live? How can we engage with those around us more deeply? How can we be more intuitive and spontaneous? Are we open to making new connections, or content with the relationships we already have?

In my experience, feeling rooted in a new place is all about establishing rituals and routines, which allow me to find emotional stillness and give me the energy to plan the next great adventure.

Short, local 'pilgrimages' often play a part in this process. Moving to Brighton in 2015 after a separation, I settled into this unfamiliar city slowly through routine and ritual. I would run along the seafront, swim between the piers, comb the shingle for hagstones (pebbles with natural holes bored through them, said to bring luck) and walk down to the beach on a Sunday evening to watch starlings swirl around the pier like smoke.

I often found myself returning to the same places, getting a feel for them in different weathers and seasons. I walked and re-walked the meanders of the River Cuckmere at Cuckmere Haven, watching geese grazing on the flats and stomping up to the rolling South Downs, which are topped with wind-bent trees. I returned time and again to nearby Hastings Old Town, picking up kiln-roasted salmon from a smokehouse in Rock-a-Nore, wandering around the tall black wooden sheds used to store fishing gear and taking a funicular ride on the East Hill Cliff Railway.

Most weekends, I would chip away at the South Downs Way – a long-distance path that follows the spine of a chalk ridge – expanding

the orbit around my new home a little further each week. Sometimes I would go with friends, but often I would be on my own, recharging on nature, just me and my squeaky left hiking boot. As I walked, I took note of the landscape. The geology of Sussex felt completely new to me. I grew up in the Pennines; I'm used to gritstone and limestone, heather moorlands and reservoirs. Sussex is chalky with crumbling cliffs, dry valleys and flint strewn fields. Ancient symbols and figures were etched into the slopes; pale mud clogged up my hiking boots. The landscape even sounded unfamiliar: skylarks rising over downland; the rasp of waves on flint pebbles; the otherworldly calls of lapwings.

To foster a sense of belonging in this new home, I retraced one particular South Downs Way path time and time again, walking from my house on the outskirts of Brighton to Pells Pool, a spring-fed lido in Lewes. Each time, I would sit at the same spot overlooking Kingston with views over windmills and inland chalk cliffs. I would observe new elements of the landscape: scores in the tussocky hillside that I had assumed were sheep tracks, I soon discovered were 'strip lynchets' or medieval ploughing lines. The ritual of walking from my front door was a balm in an otherwise difficult period of my life.

The importance of pressing pause

In a similar way, during the first UK lockdown in 2020, photographer Jim Marsden embarked on a project to tread the same local path every day. The more he walked, the less aware he became of walking, and the more aware he was of thinking. The path became his place to pause, and his space to think. Writing for *Ernest*, Jim noted: 'During the pause I became more comfortable with days filled less with doing and more with just being. Being slow. Being together as a family. Being here without worrying I should be somewhere else.'

He reflected on our discomfort with this lack of doing and wondered if it might be down to an absence of pause 'heroes' in our Western, industrialized culture. 'We revere industrialists and entrepreneurs who work tirelessly to create empires of productivity,' he wrote. 'Tales of adventurers fill our books and history lessons; people straining at the leash to be someplace other than where they were, and usually needing extraordinary mental and physical effort to get there. History's heroes are beacons of exertion and doing. But where are our heroes of being?'

Now that the world has returned to some degree of normality, familiar rhythms have returned and our pace has picked back up, it's important to keep hold of what we have learnt; to remember the truth in the 'being', rather than just the 'doing'.

Whether it's establishing meaningful rituals and routines, allowing space to pause or discovering new ways to connect and give back within our local community, bringing a slow travel mindset into our daily lives can be genuinely transformative.

Travelling slowly has much to teach us, from the importance of embracing the unexpected and letting our journeys be guided by chance encounters, to opening ourselves up to the kindness of strangers and the pleasure of connecting deeply with a landscape by moving thoughtfully through it.

But I think the most important thing to remember is that each of our journeys is unique and meaningful in its own way. So I invite you to resist the temptation to check destinations off a bucket list, and instead to follow your own whims and intuition. To travel lightly, gently and adventurously, and to explore the world (and your home ground) at your own pace.

Recommended Books, Journals & Maps

Ernest: A Journal for Enquiring Minds (Uncharted Press, 2014–); www.ernestjournal.co.uk

A Field Guide to Getting Lost, Rebecca Solnit (Canongate Books, Reprint edition, 2006)

Glasshouse Greenhouse: Haarkon's World Tour of Amazing Botanical Spaces, India Hobson and Magnus Edmondson (Pavilion, 2018)

The Green Traveller: Conscious Adventure that Doesn't Cost the Earth, Richard Hammond (Pavilion, 2022)

Grounded: How Connection with Nature Can Improve our Mental and Physical Wellbeing, Ruth Allen (Welbeck Publishing, 2021)

Herb Lester Maps: Guides to the Unexpected; herblester.com

How to Be Alone, Sara Maitland & The School of Life (Bluebird, 2014)

The Idle Traveller, Dan Kieran (AA Publishing, 2013)

The Living Mountain: A Celebration of the Cairngorm Mountains of Scotland, Nan Shepherd (Canongate Books, 2019)

Losing Eden: Why Our Minds Need the Wild, Lucy Jones (Allen Lane, 2020)

Mindful Travelling: Journeying the World, Discovering Yourself, Sarah Samuel (Leaping Hare Press, 2019)

The Natural Navigator: 10th Anniversary Edition, Tristan Gooley (Virgin Books, 2020)

A Philosophy of Walking, Frederic Gros (Verso Books, 2015)

In Praise of Slow: How a Worldwide Movement Is Challenging the Cult of Speed, Carl Honoré (Orion, 2005)

Riverwise: Meditations on Afon Teifi, Jack Smylie Wild (Parthian Books, 2020)

The Scottish Bothy Bible: The Complete Guide to Scotland's Bothies and How to Reach Them, Geoff Allan (Wild Things Publishing, 2017)

Urban Nature & National Park City Maps (London, Edinburgh, Newcastle, Glasgow, Greenwich, Amsterdam); www.urbangood.org

Walden: Or Life in the Woods, Henry David Thoreau (Vintage Classics, 2017)

Walking & Wayfinding in the Westfjords Compendium, Henry Fletcher and Jay Simpson (2022); www.wayfinding.guide

Wild Guide Scandinavia: Norway, Sweden, Iceland and Denmark, Ben Love (Wild Things Publishing, 2016)

Wild Swimming Walks (various UK locations), (Wild Things Publishing)

References

Mentioned Works

p.61 (also inspiration for text on p109, p147) *Grounded: How Connection with Nature can Improve our Mental and Physical Wellbeing,* Ruth Allen (Welbeck Publishing, Mar 2021)

p.70 *Riverwise: Meditations on Afon Teifi,* Jack Smylie Wild (Parthian Books, 2020)

p.93 'If left unchecked, a quarter of all emissions could result from flying by 2050': 'Air travel and climate change', David Suzuki Foundation; davidsuzuki.org

p.109 'Restore Your Brain with Nature', TED Talk by Dr David Strayer (2017) ted.com/talks/david_strayer_restore_your_brain_with_nature

p.110 *How to Be Alone,* Sara Maitland & The School of Life (Pan Macmillan, 2014)

P116 'We have lost the art of being alone and have gradually come to fear it', Ruth Allen, *Ernest,* issue 7

P118 'Shelter from the storm', Rich Baldwin, *Ernest,* issue 5

p.120 'Grace Denton: Baltic Residency, 2019', Grace Denton, Bothy Project; bothyproject.com

P130 *A Field Guide to Getting Lost,* Rebecca Solnit (Canongate Books, Reprint edition, 2006)

p.137 *Losing Eden: Why Our Minds Need the Wild,* Lucy Jones (Allen Lane, 2020)

p.149 'A creative pause', Jim Marsden, *Ernest,* issue 10

Provided General Inspiration

p.23 'When you don't have a destination in mind, getting lost doesn't really matter', Olivia Lee, *Ernest,* issue 8

p.40 'The tradition of *kaffemik*', Abi Whyte, *Ernest,* issue 4

p.56 *A Philosophy of Walking,* Frederic Gros (Verso Books, 2015)

p.93 'Train dreams', Dan Richards, *Ernest,* issue 10

p.130 *The Natural Navigator: 10th Anniversary Edition, Tristan Gooley* (Virgin Books, 2020)

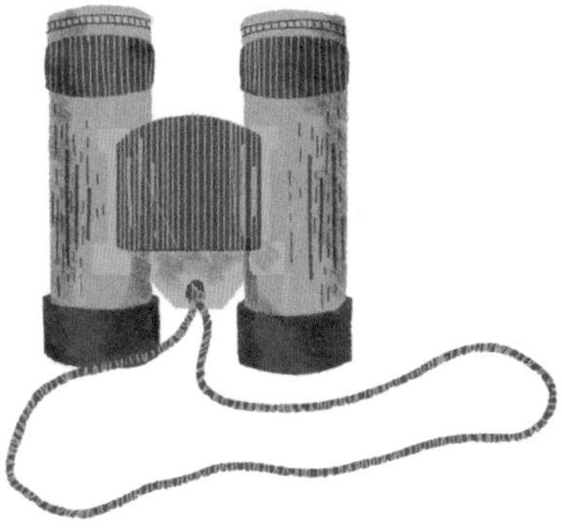

Trip Planner

Road Trips

The Seafood Trail (theseafoodtrail.com): Meandering route along the coast of Argyll, northwest Scotland, calling at crab shacks, oyster bars and seafood restaurants.

Inver at Loch Fyne (inverrestaurant.co.uk): Renovated crofter's cottage and boat store serving simply prepared fresh seafood.

The Seafood Cabin in Skipness (skipnessseafoodcabin.co.uk): Characterful waterside gem (open end May–end Sep) serving generous seafood platters.

Loch Fyne Oyster Bar and Deli at Cairndow (lochfyne.com): Drop into this loch-side deli and restaurant for the freshest seafood and smoked fish from an inhouse smokery.

Westfjords, Iceland (westfjords.is): 3–4 hour drive from Reykjavik; has an abundance of natural springs (pools 27–30°C; hot tubs 40–45°C). Entry is often free; look for donation boxes.

Krossneslaug, Norðurfjörður: Remote end-of-the-road swimming pool on Route 643 from Hólmavík (road closed for several weeks in winter). Open daily 7am–11pm, 1,000ISK.

Sharing Food

***Table d'hôtes*, France:** *Chambres d'hôtes* (B&Bs) often offer a *table d'hôte* – a home-cooked meal featuring local specialities that's served at the host's table. Enquire ahead of your stay.

Kaffemik, Greenland (visitgreenland.com): A local custom that's often held with friends and family. Stay in Greenland for a while and you might well be invited to a kaffemik.

Heimablídni, Faroe Islands (visitfaroeislands.com): Visit Faroe Islands has a list of places offering this 'home hospiality' custom.

Hanusarstova, Æðuvík, Faroe Islands (hanusarstova.com): Book a stay with Harriet and John to experience the Faroe Islands from a heartwarming local perspective.

Hiking in Picos de Europa, Spain (asturiasvertical.com): Arrange a guide in the Picos de Europa National Park with AsturiasVertical.

El Gran Sueño, Asturias (elgransueno.es/en): Refined guesthouse with a slow food philosophy, which can organise local food experiences.

Slow Food (slowfood.com): A global grassroots movement that links the pleasure of food with a commitment to community and the environment.

Long Distance Walking

Every Body Outdoors (everybodyoutdoors.co.uk): Campaigning for clothing, gear and representation for plus size bodies in the outdoors; plus mountain skills and navigation courses exclusively for plus size folk.

Unlikely Hikers (unlikelyhikers.org): US-based, diverse, anti-racist and body-liberating outdoor community featuring the under-represented outdoorsperson.

Black Girls Hike (bghuk.com): Provides a safe space for Black women to explore the outdoors. Hosts group hikes, outdoor activity days and training events to encouraging Black women to reconnect with nature.

Muslim Hikers (muslimhikers.com): Inspires Muslims to get outdoors via organised events; widening participation and increasing diversity.

Adventure Queens (adventurequeens.co.uk):
Adventure community for anyone that identifies as a woman; sharing skills, building confidence and delicately smashing barriers to the outdoors.

The Wanderlust Women
(thewanderlustwomen.co.uk):
Hiking and adventure group for Muslim women; breaking barriers and misconceptions of Muslim women.

The British Pilgrimage Trust
(britishpilgrimage.org):
Promotes pilgrimage in Britain by helping to develop and publicise new and old paths as well as the practice of pilgrimage itself.

Society of Servant Pilgrims
(societyofservantpilgrims.com):
Encourages and supports people in spiritual pilgrimage around the world.

The World Trails Network
(worldtrailsnetwork.org):
Strives to connect the diverse trails of the world; has abundant resources on long-distance trails and pilgrimage routes.

Journeys by Water

Wherry Yacht Charter (wherryyachtcharter.org):
Charter an historic wherry on the Norfolk Broads (Apr–Oct). Overnight charters come with a skipper; no sailing experience required.

Coastal Exploration Company
(coastalexplorationcompany.co.uk):
Embark on a 'Salt Marsh Sail' and let the tide carry you deep into this remarkable landscape (3–4 hours).

Discovery Island Lodge, Quadra, Vancouver Island (discovery-islands-lodge.com):
Paddle tidal rapids, explore uninhabited islands and hunt for sea stars at Discovery Island Lodge, Quadra; overnight adventures available.

Above Below (abovebelow.sc):
Pioneered cross-country swimming through their invention of the RuckRaft, an inflatable raft and drybag. Organise guided 'retreats' and publish routes and safety advice.

Adventure Uncovered (adventureuncovered.com):
Join a cycling or cross country swim; organized our 'Meandering down the Mole' expedition in collaboration with The Wild Swimming Brothers.

Another Place (another.place):
A relaxed hotel on the shores of Ullswater, Lake District. Hosts Wild Swim Camps including training, equipment and adventurous cross-country swims.

Epic Rail Journeys

Midnight Trains (midnight-trains.com):
French start-up, launching 2024, aiming to connect Paris with 12 European cities with 'hotels on rails' that freshen up the good old-fashioned sleeper train.

JR Pass (jrailpass.com):
A multi-use, discounted rail ticket giving you unlimited access to all Japan Rail National trains plus JR buses, ferries and airport transfers.

InterRail (interrail.eu):
A flexible, all-in-one rail pass that lets you explore 33 European countries by train; discounts for under-27s and over-60s.

Amtrak USA Rail Pass (amtrak.com):
This hop-on, hop-off rail pass includes 10 rides (segments) over 30 days to over 500 destinations.

The Man in Seat 61 (seat61.com):
Comprehensive hobby website aimed at inspiring people to take more rewarding journeys around Europe by train and ferry.

FEVE, Spain (renfe.com/es/es):
Narrow gauge railway along Spain's unspoilt northern coast. Independent from the main Renfe system. Timetables available online; buy tickets at the station.

Norrlandståget, Norway (sj.se/en):
Take the 18–19-hour night train from Stockholm to Narvik (also called Nattåg 94), one of many night services by Swedish operated by Swedish Railways SJ.

Simple Shelters

The Mountain Bothies Association (mountainbothies.org.uk):
Maintaining simple shelters in remote locations for all those who love wild and lonely places; browse their listings and read their Bothy Code.

Bothy Project (bothyproject.com):
Apply for a creative residency in off-grid bothy spaces to explore creativity, landscape and living simply.

Inverlonan (inverlonan.com):
Reimagining the Scottish bothy experience with architecturally designed cabins accessible by boat, foot or buggy; rough luxury, seclusion and a chance to disconnect from the day-to-day.

Alpine Club Hut in Tyrol, Austria (tyrol.com):
Browse 170+ mountain huts run by the Austrian Alpine Club, which provide hikers and walkers with protection from the elements, a warm bed and a hot meal.

Adirondack shelters (adirondack.net):
Find simple lean-to shelters (a three-sided log structure that has an overhanging roof) on trails in the Adirondack Mountains of Upstate New York.

Stay in a Boofen (German guide at wandern-saechsische-schweiz.de under 'boofenliste'):
Overnight in the open air in the Elbe Sandstone Mountains of Saxon Switzerland; these simple sleeping areas are often overhanging rocks or caves.

Urban Landscapes

The High Line, New York (thehighline.org):
Plan your visit to this verdant public park built on a historic freight rail line elevated above the streets on Manhattan's West Side (open daily 7am–7pm).

Seoul Skygarden (mvrdv.nl):
Located in the heart of Seoul, Seoullo 7017 is a former inner-city highway transformed into a 983m (0.6 miles) public park.

Englischer Garten, Munich (muenchen.de):
Visit one of Europe's largest inner-city parks, replete with beer gardens, historic follies, a Japanese tea house and surfing on the Eisbach.

San Francisco parks (sfrecpark.org):
Explore San Francisco's 220 parks, playgrounds and open spaces; browse a calendar of events, join community projects and request permits.

Copenhagen parks (visitcopenhagen.com):
Discover Assistens Kirkegård cemetery, the city's churchyard-turned-city park, plus other incredible parks such as children's bike playground in Fælledparken and Superkilen skatepark.

London National Park City (nationalparkcity.london):
A movement to improve life for everyone in London by helping everybody enjoy the city's great outdoors.

Couchsurfing (couchsurfing.com):
Connects travellers with a global network of 14 million people in 200,000 cities willing to share their worlds in profound and meaningful ways.

About the Author

Jo Tinsley

Jo is a writer, editor and independent publisher living on the edge of the Mendip Hills in Somerset, UK. She specializes in slow travel, wild swimming and outdoor lifestyle storytelling and has over 16 years' experience working in independent and specialist interest magazines. A devotee to slow journalism, Jo believes in honest and purposeful storytelling; she is the founder and editor of *Ernest*, an independent journal for enquiring minds, which is sold around the world. A keen open water swimmer and long-distance walker, Jo is never happier than when exploring a loch or bay, or when rambling over northern moorlands.
slowjo.co.uk, @SlowJoTinsley

Ernest

Ernest is an independent journal for enquiring minds. It is made for those who value surprising and meandering journeys, fuelled by curiosity rather than adrenaline and guided by chance encounters. *Ernest* is founded on the principles of slow journalism. We value honesty, integrity and down-to-earth storytelling – and a good, long read now and then.
ernestjournal.co.uk, @ernestjournal

Acknowledgements

A massive thank you to Leaping Hare Press and Quarto for publishing my first solo book. And especially to Senior Commissioning Editor Monica Perdoni, Senior Editor Laura Bulbeck and Copy Editor Robin Pridy for their support, enthusiasm and care. Writing *The Slow Traveller* has been an immense joy; it's been a pleasure to relive slow adventures undertaken over the past 20 years and to distill a slow travel philosophy that has inspired and informed so many of my own journeys.

Heartfelt thanks to Designer Tina Hobson, a long-term creative collaborator and dear friend who brought *Ernest* to splendid life and has imbued her thoughtful and timeless style within this beautiful book. Also to photographer Graeme Owsianski for accompanying me on numerous slow adventures; to Daniel Alford, Dan Cook, Jim Marsden, Colin Nicholls, Ruth Allen, Oliver Berry, Jon Stokes, Sarah Mason, Justin Glynn, Rich Baldwin, Andrew Ridley, India and Magnus of Haarkon, and to all of the photographers who shared their images within these pages; plus artist Aidan Meighan for his super illustrations.

I would also like to thank my partner, Sam, whose continued support, grounding nature and kindness has allowed me headspace to write while we raise an adventurous little one. Finally, I would like to dedicate this book to my dad, Mark, who instilled in me an enthusiasm for train travel and long-distance walking from a young age. Dad sadly passed away while I was writing this book, but his memory lives on in my undiminished desire to explore the world under my own steam, and with care – a passion I share with my toddler daughter, a champion footpath stomper and steam train enthusiast, with an enviable sense of curiosity and wonder in the world.

Contributors

The Illustrator:

Aidan Meighan is an illustrator and cartographer living in Somerset, with ten years' experience drawing for travel and lifestyle books and magazines. With a passion for nature and the outdoors, he has found a distinctive style of design for his work, and has drawn and mapped many beautiful places around the world.
whereaboutsmaps.com; @whereaboutsmaps

The Photographers:

Daniel Alford is a Welsh editorial and commercial photographer/filmmaker who specializes in travel and natural history.
danielalford.co.uk; @danielalford_

Ruth Allen is an Embodied Psychotherapist specializing in outdoor practice, and Author of *Grounded*. She lives and works on the edge of the Peak District, and is currently writing her second book, *Weathering*.
whitepeakwellbeing.com; @whitepeak_ruth

Rich Baldwin is a fell runner, who is happiest running up and down hills, sleeping in a bivi bag and floating about on lochs on his packraft. When he's not doing that he lives in the Midlands and works full time in a psychiatric hospital, working with people who have problems with addiction.
@runridesleepoutside

Oliver Berry is a writer, photographer and filmmaker, specializing in travel, nature and the great outdoors. His work has been featured by Lonely Planet, the BBC, the *Guardian*, *The Times*, *Kinfolk*, *Ernest* and many other renowned publications.
oliverberry.com; @olivertomberry

Dan Cook shares his love of the outdoors through his award-winning photography, capturing landscapes, journeys and smaller details that tell stories from days spent wandering in locations across the globe. Dan is happiest with a camera in hand and a long walk ahead, ideally with a pub at the end.
danscape.co; @dan_scape

Justin Glynn is a photographer and filmmaker based in Dorset, UK, with a decade of experience in the industry, specializing in both landscape and corporate work. Justin's work is a perfect blend of art and storytelling, and his passion for capturing the beauty of the natural world and the unique stories of businesses and individuals has earned him a reputation for creating stunning and impactful content.
harbourmedia.co.uk; @harbour_media

Haarkon: In 2015 India and Magnus began documenting the journeys they made whilst on assignment as professional photographers. They created Haarkon.co.uk as a way to record their images, thoughts, and experiences. They make books and small paper goods inspired by their ever-changing surroundings.
Haarkon.co.uk

Jim Marsden was born in the Rossendale Valley, Lancashire and grew up with a love of the landscape and a curiosity for people. He uses this to create work for clients and his own side projects.
iamjim.co.uk; @jimmarsdenphotography

Sarah Mason is a filmmaker and photographer living in West Yorkshire with her wife and daughter. She is drawn to telling quiet, honest stories about the things that make us who we are. She works with artists, makers and families, as well as creating brand campaigns.
sarahmasonphotography.co.uk;
@sarahmasonfilmmakeruk

Colin Nicholls is a freelance photographer and filmmaker based in Hereford, UK, specializing in documentary style images. His clean and crisp style aims to reflect the reality of his subject matter while drawing the viewer in to see what else there is to explore.
@colinnichollsphotography

Graeme Owsianski is a lifestyle, editorial and travel photographer from Vancouver Island, Canada.
@graeme_o

Andrew Ridley is a photographer from the North East of England. His interest in a subject lies in its details. He wants to offer newness in places and objects you may have walked past a hundred times. In his landscapes, he aims to pay close attention to light, texture, colour, and to find the finest vantage point to offer vast scenes a certain intimacy.
aridleyphotography.com

Jonathan Stokes' photography career has seen him work in the UK and across five continents. He approaches his subject with the desire to create 'big pictures': natural shots, rich in detail, depth and texture. Inspired by a love of cinema, and a passion for exploring the human and natural world, Jon always works to tell stories sympathetically, but with a striking visual style.
jonathanstokesphotography.com;
@jonathanstokesphoto

Thanks also to:
Adventure Uncovered: ***adventureuncovered.com;*** **Tom Bailey, *Trail* magazine; Above Below:** ***abovebelow.sc;*** **Sam and Tina Hobson.**

Credits

Front cover: *Ladybower, Peak District, UK:* © 2023 Haarkon

Back cover top & 10–11 *Faroe:* © 2023 Graeme Owsianski. **Back cover bottom & 15** *Madeira:* © 2023 Daniel Cook.

Interiors:
All illustrations by Aidan Meighan.

Photographs copyright © 2023 the following: **4** *Madeira:* Daniel Cook; **5t** *Madeira:* Daniel Cook; **5b** *Amsterdam, Netherlands:* Haarkon; **6** *Westfjords, Iceland:* Graeme Owsianski; **9** *Faroe:* Graeme Owsianski; **17** *Yosemite, USA:* Haarkon; **18** *Galapagos:* Graeme Owsianski; **20–21** *Yorkshire Moors, UK:* Daniel Alford; **22** *Yorkshire Moors, UK:* Daniel Alford; **23** *East Anglia, UK:* Colin Nicholls; **25 (all)** *Westfjords, Iceland:* Graeme Owsianski; **26** *Madeira:* Daniel Cook; **27** *Settle, North Yorkshire UK:* Ruth Allen; **29tl** *Isles of Scilly, UK:* Oliver Berry / oliverberry.com; **29tr** *Scottish Highlands, UK:* Sarah Mason; **29br** *Cloud Forest, Ecuador:* Graeme Owsianski; **29bl** *East Anglia, UK:* Colin Nicholls; **30–31** *Pyrenées, France:* Sam Hobson; **32** *Scottish Highlands, UK:* Sarah Mason; **33** *East Anglia, UK:* Colin Nicholls; **34** *Snowdonia, Wales:* Ruth Allen; **35** *Kennedy Lake, British Columbia, Canada:* Graeme Owsianski; **38** *British Columbia, Canada:* Graeme Owsianski; **39** *Faroe:* Graeme Owsianski; **41 (all)** *Greenland:* Daniel Alford; **42 (all)** *Old Harry Rock, Dorset, UK:* Justin Glynn– Harbour Media; **44** *Asturias, Spain:* Colin Nicholls; **45** *Siem Reap, Cambodia:* Haarkon; **46** *Faroe:* Graeme Owsianski; **47 (all)** *Faroe:* Graeme Owsianski; **49** *Asturias, Spain:* Ruth Allen; **50** *Asturias, Spain:* Ruth Allen; **51 (all)** *Asturias, Spain:* Ruth Allen; **54** *Dolomites, Italy:* Daniel Cook; **55** *Madeira:* Daniel Cook; **57tl** *Southdowns, UK:* Jim Marsden; **57tr** *East Anglia, UK:* Colin Nicholls; **57bl** *East Anglia, UK:* Colin Nicholls; **57br** *East Anglia, UK:* Colin Nicholls; **58–59** *Teifi, Wales, UK:* Daniel Alford; **60** *Madeira:* Daniel Cook; **63** *Asturias, Spain:* Ruth Allen; **64** *Dartmoor, UK:* Jim Marsden; **65** *Madeira:* Daniel Cook; **66–67** *Monknash, South Wales, UK:* Daniel Alford; **68** *Romania:* Ruth Allen (2022); **69** *Kyoto, Japan:* Haarkon; **71 (all)** *Teifi, Wales, UK:* Daniel Alford; **72** *Isles of Scilly, UK:* Oliver Berry / oliverberry.com; **73** *Poland:* Daniel Cook; **76** Wroxham, Norfolk Broads, UK: Jonathan Stokes Photography; **77** *Wroxham, Norfolk Broads, UK:* Jonathan Stokes Photography; **79tl** *Wroxham, Norfolk Broads, UK:* Jonathan Stokes Photography; **79tr** *How Hill, Norfolk Broads, UK:* Jonathan Stokes Photography; **79b** *Norfolk Broads, UK:* Jonathan Stokes Photography; **80** *Wroxham, Norfolk Broads, UK:* Jonathan Stokes Photography; **82–83** *British Columbia, Canada:* Graeme Owsianski; **85 (all)** *British Columbia, Canada:* Graeme Owsianski; **86** *Lake District, UK:* Colin Nicholls; **87** *Lake District, UK:* Colin Nicholls; **89tl** *River Mole, UK:* Adventure Uncovered; **89tr** *Lake District, UK:* Colin Nicholls; **89b** *Lake District, UK:* Tom Bailey, *Trail* magazine; **92** *Grindelwald, Switzerland:* Daniel Cook; **93** *Cloud Forest, Ecuador:* Graeme Owsianski; **95tl** *Cornwall, UK:* Daniel Cook; **95b** *Cornwall, UK:* Daniel Cook; **95tr** *beach artist Sean Cocoran on Kilmurrin Cove, Ireland:* Daniel Alford; **96–97** *California, USA:* Haarkon; **98** *Grindelwald, Switzerland:* Daniel Cook; **101** *Embsay Railway Station, North Yorkshire, UK:* Andrew Ridley Photography; **102** *Embsay & Bolton Abbey Railway, UK:* Andrew Ridley Photography; **103** *Embsay & Bolton Abbey Railway, UK:* Andrew Ridley Photography; **105** *Hakone, Japan:* Haarkon; **108** *Scotland:* Daniel Cook; **111** *Lake District, UK:* Daniel Cook; **112–113** *Scottish Highlands, UK:* Sarah Mason; **114** *Snowdonia, UK:* Colin Nicholls; **115** *Cadair Idris, Snowdonia, Wales, UK:* Daniel Alford; **117t** *Port Gobhlaig, Isle of Skye, Scotland:* Daniel Cook; **117b** *Scottish Highlands, UK:* Rich Baldwin; **119** *Lake District, UK:* Daniel Cook; **120** *Scottish Highlands, UK:* Sarah Mason; **121t** *Northern Lights above Tryfan, Snowdonia, Wales, UK:* Daniel Alford; **121bl** *Finland:* Ruth Allen; **121br** *Finland:* Ruth Allen; **124** *Brighton, UK:* Jim Marsden; **125** *Tokyo, Japan:* Haarkon; **127tl** *Japan:* Haarkon; **127tr** *Amsterdam, Netherlands:* Haarkon; **127b** *Brighton, UK:* Jim Marsden; **128** *Bristol, UK:* Jim Marsden; **131** *Singapore:* Haarkon; **132–133** *Tokyo, Japan:* Haarkon; **134** *Avebury, UK:* Tina Hobson; **135** *Amsterdam, Netherlands:* Haarkon; **136** *San Francisco, USA:* Haarkon; **137** *London, UK:* Haarkon; **138** *NYC, USA:* Haarkon; **139** *NYC, USA:* Haarkon; **142** *Brighton, UK:* Jim Marsden; **145** *Seven Sisters, East Sussex, UK:* Jim Marsden; **146** *East Anglia, UK:* Colin Nicholls; **148t** *Brighton, UK:* Jim Marsden; **148b** *East Anglia, UK:* Colin Nicholls; **151** *East Anglia, UK:* Colin Nicholls.